MONTGOMERY COLLEGE LIBRARY
GERMANTOWN CAMPUS

JEAN-PAUL SARTRE

# MODERN MASTERS

ALBERT CAMUS / Conor Cruise O'Brien
FRANTZ FANON / David Caute
HERBERT MARCUSE / Alasdair MacIntyre
CHE GUEVARA / Andrew Sinclair
LUDWIG WITTGENSTEIN / David Pears
GEORGE LUKÁCS / George Lichtheim
NOAM CHOMSKY / John Lyons
JAMES JOYCE / John Gross
MARSHALL MCLUHAN / Jonathan Miller
GEORGE ORWELL / Raymond Williams
SIGMUND FREUD / Richard Wollheim
WILLIAM BUTLER YEATS / Denis Donoghue
WILHELM REICH / Charles Rycroft
MOHANDAS GANDHI / George Woodcock
BERTRAND RUSSELL / A. J. Ayer
NORMAN MAILER / Richard Poirier

# ALREADY PUBLISHED

V. I. LENIN / Robert Conquest
EINSTEIN / Jeremy Bernstein
C. G. JUNG / Anthony Storr
D. H. LAWRENCE / Frank Kermode
KARL POPPER / Bryan Magee
SAMUEL BECKETT / A. Alvarez
R. D. LAING / Edgar Z. Friedenberg
MAX WEBER / Donald G. MacRae
MARCEL PROUST / Roger Shattuck
CLAUDE LÉVI-STRAUSS (*Rev. Ed.*) / Edmund Leach
LE CORBUSIER / Stephen Gardiner
ARNOLD SCHOENBERG / Charles Rosen
FRANZ KAFKA / Erich Heller
KARL MARX / David McLellan
T. S. ELIOT / Stephen Spender

MODERN MASTERS

EDITED BY frank kermode

# jean-paul sartre

## arthur c. danto

NEW YORK | THE VIKING PRESS

Copyright © 1975 by Arthur C. Danto

All rights reserved

Published in 1975 in a hardbound and paperbound edition by
The Viking Press, Inc. 625 Madison Avenue,
New York, N.Y. 10022

LIBRARY OF CONGRESS CATALOGING IN PUBLICATION DATA
Danto, Arthur Coleman, 1924–
Jean-Paul Sartre.

(Modern masters)
Bibliography: p.
Includes index.
1. Sartre, Jean Paul, 1905–
B2430.S34D32     194      75-19019
ISBN 0-670-40630-9
ISBN 0-670-01990-9 pbk.

Printed in U.S.A.

For ROBERT DENOON CUMMING
and JAMES W. WALSH

# PREFACE

A scribbler from childhood, as he tells us in his autobiography, Sartre's literary output has been stupendous, as much for the originality and variety of its production as for the sheer weight of its many volumes: to have written that much at all is an achievement, apart from so much of it being good or even great. It is difficult to think of a comparable corpus: the dramatic works alone would insure him a place in theatrical history; novelists have been considered important none of whose works is on a plane with *Nausea*; the criticism and biographical writings put Sartre in the first echelons of these possibly less luminous genres. And his life has been one of the exemplary lives, a paradigm of commitment and courage as well as of creativity, full of positions taken and fine causes promoted and hideous ones opposed, an articulated if sometimes futile conscience and moral witness against the outrage of twentieth-century history. An attractive personality, generous and decent, ironic and brilliant, skeptical and enthusiastic, Parisian to the core, committed in love and friendship to the values of freedom and fidelity—even as a character, just as a man, Sartre merits memorialization and admiration. But the singularities of his wider literary contribution, his person and his life, are overshadowed, to my mind, by his extraordinary philosophical craft. The Sartrian system, for its scope and ingenuity, its architectural daring and logical responsibility, its dialectical strengths and human relevance, and for the totality of its vision, is located in the same exalted category, the highest of its kind, as those of Plato and Descartes, Spinoza and Kant, Hegel and Russell, to cite most of his exiguous peers. His polyvalent genius is most centrally manifested in this system, and I have therefore made it central in this book, which attempts its synoptic and sympathetic reconstruction, for it is this, I believe, which is the most important and least accessible and most widely misappreciated of all that he has done. It is misappreciated most particularly, I think, by other philosophers, who, unless they are mere enthusiasts, dismiss his work as willfully obscure, or nonsensical, or derivative.

Obscure at times Sartre certainly is, and not merely in consequence of the inherently difficult ideas he has endeavored to express—though by comparison with contemporary French philosophical writers, addressing immeasurably more tractable notions, even the darkest pages of *Being and Nothingness* or the *Critique de la raison dialectique* have an almost Cartesian transparency. *Being and Nothingness*, which I count a masterpiece and place at the center of my exposition (though Sartre himself no longer regards it central in his thought), is undeniably repetitious and portentous, and suffers in many of its major formulations less from

*Preface* | *xi*

muddled expression than a kind of perverse verbal wit, a kind of willed contrariety of usage, which may seem to come to the same thing. Thus, for only one example, Sartre declares that conscious beings, in contrast with mere objects, "are what they are not and are not what they are." This sounds if not obscure then certainly nonsensical, insofar as it suggests that conscious beings fall outside the scope of the Principle of Identity, which because it is a logical truth can have no consistent exceptions, and the formula is accordingly incoherent just on formal grounds. Nevertheless, as we shall see, the statement condenses and dramatizes a set of structures Sartre supposes he has found at the conceptual heart of consciousness, and with the least measure of patience and toleration it is possible not only to work out a coherent paraphrase but to appreciate the degree to which what he says may after all be true. And so with all the inverted slogans of that marvelous book, whose verbal surface alone they disfigure if they disfigure even that. But apart from failures in logical coherence, I know of no criterion of nonsense by which that book or any can be rendered inscrutable. There is, to be sure, the ravaged Criterion of Non-Verifiability which, when it appeared a generation ago to be a shining sword, was cleverly applied by positivistic knights to slay existentialism. As it happens, the solitary victim of the Non-Verifiability Criterion was itself, and existentialism remains as little touched by it as metaphysics generally, to be judged by criteria more nearly applicable to philosophy than to empirical science (which in any case would have been as vulnerable to the Criterion as the foggiest pages of Heidegger). My book, meanwhile, will serve, I hope, to repudiate the charge of unoriginality. Sartre has, certainly, his debts, pre-eminently to Heidegger and to Husserl. But what he has taken he has transfigured, and the influences upon him are conserved only by being transcended in a system of singular novelty and imagination. No one, I believe, could have deduced the Sartrian modulations of Husserl's analysis of consciousness or Heidegger's conception of nothingness.

My approach is structural and synchronic, treating Sartre's system timelessly, disregarding in favor of logical reconstruction such interesting questions as the development of the system in Sartre's thought, and the system's location in the history of philosophy. After all, we need some clear sense of the shape of the product before we can relevantly trace the stages of its evolution, and in a certain sense the relevant history of a philosophical system is logically internal to the system itself, since it determines which earlier philosophies are to be reckoned amongst its causes. *We* define who our predecessors are, and create our own histories as effects of what we do.

I have described five sorts of structures in as many chapters: the relationship between reality and our representations of it; the parities between language and consciousness from the perspective of ontological commitment; the relationship between the world as it may be in itself and as it is structured through our interventions as engaged beings; the conceptual interdependence of the self and other selves; and the connections between factual beliefs and systems of value. My choice of these topics has been determined not only through the fact that they dominate Sartre's philosophy but because each raises questions of such wide and current philosophical interest that the pertinence of his thought to contemporary speculation and analysis—and vice versa—may be most perspicuously demonstrated through them. My aim in this book is ecumenical as well as expository and critical. The ideologized division of philosophers into analysts on one side and existentialists or phenomenologists on the other is silly and destructive. For we are all doing the same thing, pursuing all the same structures, whether the ostensible topic of our investigation is language or consciousness. And to show this is to bring a further, essential degree of self-consciousness to the philosophical undertaking as a whole.

Finally, and more personally, it is not just because it is inherently interesting and immediately pertinent that I composed this study of the philosophy of Jean-Paul Sartre. It is because as a philosophical writer myself I am heavily in his debt. Though the main things I have written are, in style and temper, within the analytical movement, to which I owe an allegiance, I have quarried Sartre's work like a Barbarini over the years, taken fragments of his thought which I would never, I am certain, have been able to think of by myself, and incorporated them as elements in my own structures, whatever their merits. So in an internal way he is part of my own history and world, and this is meant to be an acknowledgment of my obligation as well as of my admiration.

I am grateful to the Council in Humanities of Columbia University for a summer stipend which took me to Paris to complete the inquiries this book and some collateral papers represent, and to the generosity of The Rockefeller Foundation, which by an invitation to its Study Center in Bellagio enabled me to complete the writing under the most ideal circumstances imaginable.

A. C. D.

*New York–Paris–Bellagio, 1974*

Because this book is addressed, in addition to the general literary public, to two sets of philosophical readers not always on speaking terms, every chapter has two titles, one in the idiom of each camp. The system of bititularity may be taken in the spirit of a translational dictionary. Obviously the connotative range of corresponding terms in no two languages will exactly coincide, since what they designate may play different roles in the cultures with which the languages go, but enough conceptual community remains for interlinguistic discourse to be feasible. The meanings of terms in the existentialist and nonexistentialist vocabularies are no more radically untranslatable into one another than those, say, in English and French.

CONTENTS

Preface xi

 i / Absurdity: or, Language and Existence 1

 ii / Nothingness: or, Consciousness and Ontology 38

iii / Engagement: or, Knowledge, Action, and the World 82

 iv / Shame: or, the Problem of Other Minds 107

  v / Anguish: or, Factual Beliefs and Moral Attitudes 147

Sartre's Life: A Biographical Note 163

Short Bibliography 167

Index 171

Absurdity: or, Language and Existence

# 1

Sartre's great philosophical novel *Nausea* (1938) is a sustained reflection on the relationships and ultimately the discrepancies between the world and our ways of representing it, and each major character is defined through his deep belief that reality has the structures which instead belong, he comes to realize, to the several ways he organizes it. Thus the Autodidact, a pathetic and hopeless figure, devotes himself to the mastery of the whole of knowledge by reading alphabetically through a provincial library, an enterprise which implies a view that the world itself is articulated essentially the way an encyclopedia is (a not altogether eccentric view if we think that it was precisely the *Encyclopédie* of Diderot which was the great literary achievement of the Age of Reason, and which expressed, less through its contents than the manner of their arrangement, the outlook on the world of the class for which it spoke: the *Encyclopédie* meant to house the whole of knowledge, put in exactly alphabetical order). The hero's lost and then found mistress, Anny, seeks to live her life in terms of "perfect moments," as though living had the structure of its poetical representations, and she finds her lover clumsy and inadequate by reference to criteria of perfection which have at best an application in art rather than life. The hero, Roquentin, becomes aware, at a critical moment, that he has "had no adventures," not because his life has been singularly monotonous—it has not been—but because the concept of "adventure" applies to the narrative organization of life rather than to the living of it: "For the most banal event to become an adventure, all one must do is start telling about it,"[1] he notes in his journal. "That is what deceives people: a man is always a teller of stories, he lives surrounded by his stories and the stories of others, he sees everything which happens to him through these stories; and he tries to live his life as if it were a story he was telling." He had wanted the moments of his life to follow one another and order themselves like a life remembered, he says, but "I might as well try to catch time by the tail."[2] You have to choose, he decides, "Live or tell." But the structures of telling are utterly discordant with the immediate experience of life, or distort it if we try to live it that way. And this has to be a shattering insight to a hero whose project is, as Roquentin's was, that of a historian, or worse a biographer, confined to the provincial bleakness of Bouville

---

[1] *Nausea*, trans. Lloyd Alexander, p. 56. I refer the reader to the translation by Alexander, though I have altered it at points to bring it more in line with the original text as I perceive it.

[2] *Ibid.*, p. 58.

(literally, Mudville), consulting archives out of which he intends to reconstitute the life of a certain Monsieur Rollebon, a diplomat long dead; for in the very telling of the story of Rollebon's (or anyone's) life, he will falsify its reality, as he falsifies his own the moment he thinks of it narratively.

The structure of *Nausea* in a way anticipates the disillusionment this thought brings, since it has the form of a journal in which Roquentin sets down the things that happen to him day by day—as though the only adequate description of a life would be as disconnected and merely sequential as daily living is. Sartre did not always adhere to this view. In the *Critique de la raison dialectique*, written twenty years later, it was precisely his aim to see if history did not indeed have a narrative structure, in which events were internally related to one another in reality and not just in their description, fitting into objective and total structures we discovered and did not just impose upon them, instead of standing in the external and atomistic relationships of a mere chronicle. But in that strange, long, repetitious, and obscure work, it is not easy to separate the treatment of the problem from the problem treated, as if the writing of the book were its own subject and the philosophy of history merely an excuse for wrestling with it. The *Critique* is a jungle, more of words than even of prose, wildly in need of editorial pruning and discipline, *if* we think of it as a treatise rather than the attempt to write a treatise. But if it is the latter, then its record of the false starts, its obsessive return to badly developed but still promising starting points, its breakthroughs, reconsiderations, hesitations, and qualifications are all essential—as in a drawing by Rembrandt in which the penciled lines reveal less a form than the searching for it, and the artistic labor is not just inseparable from the work but is the work. So we don't so much read the *Critique* as relive the writing of it. And something like this is true of *Nausea* as well.

The central revelation of the failure of fit between language and reality comes at the climactic moment in the novel-journal in which the meaning is discovered of that odd, undiagnosed nausea, which is the disturbing stimulus to which writing the journal is the response of an essentially literary man. It is the moment at which Roquentin sustains an almost mystical encounter with the twisted, black roots of an ancient chestnut tree in a park in Bouville—in this instance the tree of the knowledge of language and truth—where he recognizes that the distance between the tree and any description of it is hopeless, and cannot be overcome by more words, that there is no way in which this tree (or anything) can be transformed, as it were, into language. The tree is logically external to words as words, it refuses to be swallowed by words, and words, to continue the metaphor, choke in the attempt to ingest it. So nausea is the vivid pathological symbol of the utter externality between words and things. "The root of the chestnut tree sank into the ground beneath my bench. I couldn't remember it was a root any more. Words had vanished, and with them the meanings of things, the way things are to be used, the feeble points of reference which men have traced on their surface."[3] This was a philosophical and indeed a kind of mystical vision, but it would be available only to someone who had first supposed that the orders of discourse and the orders of things were one, and that reality had as its resident armatures just that network of connections which belong to speech instead. As if, if it did not have *that* structure, it had not

[3] *Ibid.*, pp. 170–71.

## Absurdity: or, Language and Existence | 5

any. "The root, the park gates, the bench, the sparse bits of grass, all that had vanished: the diversity of things, their individuality, were only an appearance, a varnish. This varnish had melted, leaving soft, monstrous lumps, in naked disorder, with a frightful and obscure nakedness."[4]

The perception of reality which the striking, frightening vision allegedly dissolves is one we must carefully describe, for it will become important in our exposition of Sartre's philosophy. Essentially, it is the view, that in order for reality to be described it must already have the structures of language itself, as though language could fit the world only if the two were costructural, like hand and glove, or an object and its mirror image. We find this view in many philosophers, perhaps implicitly in most philosophers, but it is expressed most perspicuously in the early philosophy of Wittgenstein, according to whom sentences, in the ideal case, are *pictures* of facts whose forms they show; the world itself is a set of facts and not things; so that the logical shape of the basic units of reality are of a piece with the logical shape of the sentences which represent them, community of logical form being the precondition for representational adequacy. It would come as a deeply disturbing revelation to someone who thought this way, or it could come as a liberating insight (as it did to Wittgenstein), to realize that the world lacks anything like logical form, that logical form belongs to language, and that one errs in supposing that logical form belongs to reality. In the light of what had heretofore been deemed a necessary condition for language to represent the world, this position would entail the argument that since this condition fails, language cannot represent

[4] *Ibid.*, pp. 171–72.

the world at all, and that the world as it really is lies beyond the power of language to say. Wittgenstein, in his later philosophy, proposed in effect that it was a mistake to think of language as primarily descriptive at all; one must think of it rather as an instrument for the facilitation of forms of life. But if this possibility is not appreciated, the perception of the agrammaticality of nature can precipitate the sort of crisis of descriptive impotency felt by Roquentin. Of course, the real question is whether anything remotely like the supposed condition is necessary after all. Only someone who believed it was would fall into a swoon of semantical nihilism of the sort which seizes Roquentin in the park. It is the falsity of this philosophy of language which his nausea dimly prefigures, and which comes to consciousness before the chestnut tree.

Roquentin's commentary on the experience is singularly philosophical. In having thought, for instance, that the sea was green or that a certain white patch in the sky was a gull, "I was thinking of properties," he writes. "I was telling myself that the sea belonged to the class of green objects, or that green was one of the qualities of the sea."[5] And what is wrong with this, unless there is something wrong in supposing the world to contain real counterparts to what are marked in language as subjects and predicates? But now what has happened is that the world "has lost the harmless look of an abstract category: it was the dough out of which things were made." Briefly, Roquentin concludes, he was not seeing the world as it is, but rather through the shaping structures of language, and now that it has occurred to him that

---

[5] *Ibid.* Sartre uses the word *appartenance*, which I deem it better to render as "properties," following Cumming in *The Philosophy of Jean-Paul Sartre*, p. 60, than as the literal "belonging," as in Alexander.

*Absurdity: or, Language and Existence* | 7

these structures have no objective correlates, he thinks he is forced to attribute to the world exactly the absence of any structures at all—where he might instead have concluded not that it lacks structure but that it lacks these *sorts* of structures, and have sought for a sounder metaphysics of speech. And instead of despairing at our incapacity to "put things into words," he might rather have rethought the nature of the connection.

There is a more traditional way of viewing Roquentin's (or, really, Sartre's) linguistic agonies here, and it is tied up with a notion of "existence." For after all it is existence which he realizes, or believes he realizes, cannot be put into words, and it is exactly in these terms that he phrases the content of his experience: "existence had suddenly unveiled itself."[6] This is the philosophical tradition in which the notions of *existence* and *essence* are counterposed, a tradition which leads back to Aristotle through the scholastic philosophy of the high Middle Ages from the academic philosophy of the French universities in which Sartre was educated. It was intellectually a live tradition for him, even if it was his philosophical style to pervert the traditional distinctions to his own expository ends—as when he says, in his famous lecture "Existentialism Is a Humanism," that existence "precedes" essence, or at least in the case of man, that we have an existence but not an essence, that there is no common human nature which men everywhere and always exemplify, no set of conditions necessary and sufficient through which human beings are defined (or they are defined through the fact that they are indefinable in those sorts of terms). Sartre, however innovative his thought and vocabulary, has

[6] *Ibid.*

always worked, even as a Marxist but certainly as an existentialist, within the dry array of distinctions of a largely scholastic metaphysics, and we only can appreciate the originality of his thought with reference to the schemes he has to distort in order to express it. And, as we shall see in a moment, he reacts with a dramatized shock to theses which other philosophers might coolly accept in their studies and flatly expound in their classrooms: it is the response of someone discovering that a philosophy is false which he had first supposed true the way in which science is, who believes in effect that philosophies are things we live by, rather than merely study as abstract edifices of conceptual architecture. This is nowhere more evident than in Roquentin's intense reaction to the thought that the existence of something is not part of its essence, that the existence of things is never entailed by their definition: a notion the academic philosopher might merely teach. I shall briefly sketch the background of this thought, and then return to Sartre's exceedingly colorful interpretation of it.

The scholastics believed that there were certain terms which, if true of a thing, were *essentially* true of it, in the sense that the thing *must have* the properties ascribed to it by the terms, if it were to be the kind of thing it was said to be. By contrast, there were terms which were only accidentally true of a thing, in the sense that the latter would remain the kinds of thing it was, whether it had the ascribed property or not. The first sort of term determined the "essence" of the thing, and it was then a matter of necessity that a thing of a given kind have those properties. Suppose, merely for illustration, that we accept the shopworn definition of man as a rational animal. Then nothing can both be

## Absurdity: or, Language and Existence | 9

human and nonrational, and rationality belongs accordingly to the essence of humankind. Actual men have many qualities other than the essential ones on this view: some are clever, others are silly, some are physically powerful, some are physically flawed. It may be true of a man *m* that he is blind, but not necessarily true of him as a *man* that he is so, it being no part of our essence that we should have or lack vision. So this would be an accidental fact. It would then be the belief that we understand things when we know what their essences are, and essences are expressed in what are called "real definitions." The outcome of such inquiries as those we find in the Platonic dialogues would be real definitions in this sense: discoveries of the essence of love or justice or friendship or whatever. What Kant spoke of as analytical judgments are akin to this ideal, these being judgments which, if true, are so not in virtue of their form (as logical truths are) or in terms of the way the world happens to be (since it could have been different) but rather through the meanings of the terms with which they are expressed. Thus, for Kant, "All bodies are spatially extended" is analytically true while "All bodies have weight" is not, weightless bodies being a not incoherent notion, even if bodies all in fact weigh something. So spatial extension, in this tradition, would pertain to the essence of bodies, and weight would be relegated to mere accident.

Thinkability, necessity, contingency, meaning, truth, and accidentality—ponderous concepts all—intersect in the doctrine of essences; it is indeed one of those dense conceptual knots in and out of which almost every thread of philosophical thought is wound, and in terms of which almost the whole of philosophical thinking can be expressed. We hardly can do more than indicate the complexities here in passing, but neither can we broach the philosophical concept of existence save with reference to it, for the traditional teaching was that the existence of things did not form part of their essence, and it is this thought which Sartre means to express in his own way through the discomforts of Roquentin and, later, directly in his own philosophy. What the teaching implies is that, in whatever way it is, for example, unthinkable that something should be human without being rational or a body without being extended, it is *always* thinkable that there should exist neither men nor bodies; there always are possible worlds in which there are no men or material objects at all—worlds of pure number, say, or worlds made up of someone's thoughts. But in that tradition, *one* concept stands as an exception, and it is illuminating for Sartre's philosophy to mention it here. This would be the concept of God, who exists necessarily, *his* existence being his essence; this collapse of the distinction between essence and existence lies at the heart of one of the most famous proofs of God, Anselm's celebrated Ontological Argument, according to which the nonexistence of God, in contrast with the nonexistence of any other being, is wholly unthinkable. But this mooted example apart, the received view always was, as Hume put it, that we can deny the existence of anything whatever without penalty of incoherence, even if in many cases we shall be (accidentally) wrong.

And this, at last, is almost precisely the gist of Roquentin's vision: existence is always something literally *extra*, something unconstrained by any necessity of concept or thought. Hence the existence of things is always logically superfluous, and never part of the concept we may apply to them. Superfluous or, as Sartre puts it, *de trop:* "*Superfluous*, the chestnut tree there, in front of me, a little to the left. *Superfluous*, the Velleda.

## Absurdity: or, Language and Existence | 11

And I, myself—soft, weak, obscene, digesting, juggling with dismal thoughts—*I, too, am superfluous.*"[7] The existence of each thing, ourselves included, is radically unnecessary, which is what the concept of superfluity connotes, but which, embedded as it is in the relevant philosophical structures, has also the connotation of being a merely accidental truth, something which is true *as it happens* but which could have been otherwise. No one could deduce from its description that there is a world or what the world might contain.

It is important that we appreciate the way in which Sartre embroiders poetically and allusively on a term like "superfluity," which has for him in fact a strict philosophical sense. And we may see this even more clearly through the even more striking use he makes of a term with which his philosophy, in the popular mind, is virtually synonymous, namely, "absurdity." "The word 'absurdity' is emerging under my pen," Roquentin writes in his journal, "and without formulating anything clearly, I understood that I had found the clue to Existence, the clue to my Nauseas, to my own life."[8]

Let me first attempt the clear formulation which Roquentin goes on to lyricize. My absurdity, like that of the chestnut tree and indeed of anything, lies in our common superfluousness, in the fact that none of our existences is necessitated by our essences (all the more so if we have no essences), in the fact that we do not exist necessarily or, more exactly, that we are not God, construed medievally as *ens realissimum*, the one being whose existence is a requirement of its concept. Later, in *Being and Nothingness*, Sartre will suppose it a generalized quest of human beings to be like God, to

[7] *Ibid.*, p. 173.
[8] *Ibid.*, pp. 173, 174.

contain each within his being the logical guarantee of himself. And this, Sartre will argue, or assume without argumentation, is impossible; man, who cannot abandon a project which he also cannot fulfill, is doomed to a logical failure and so, in a favorite Sartrian phrase, is a "futile passion." For we are hopelessly contingent beings, thrown, as Heidegger would say, into a world which could logically have existed without us, being *itself* radically contingent at every point. And this is what absurdity deeply means: not silly or meaningless or insequential, but contingent. And one will experience this with a metaphysical urgency only to the degree that one thinks of what a nonabsurd thing would be, or a nonabsurd world, namely one which satisfies a concept of logical or near-logical necessity. Sartre's view of reality is in effect exactly Hume's, but dramatized by means of a charged term with a certain life of its own, which easily slips free of the philosophical tethers that give it its original sense and allows itself to be used as a kind of slogan, with all the associations absurdity has acquired in the contexts of literature, and as a pretext for that chic sort of despair to which the life of the literary café is so hospitable. And this, as we shall see over and over, is typical of the lexical perversities through which Sartre expresses his genius: energized terms like dread and anguish, engagement and nothingness, nausea and shame, terms whose central meaning is quite sober when introduced through the contexts of argument and system which Sartre as philosopher develops, spill beyond these into affective and emotional spaces that Sartre as a literary person exploits.

There is another dimension to the concept of superfluity—of logical excess—which we may enter by considering some of the sorts of things Roquentin feels *not*

## Absurdity: or, Language and Existence | 13

to be absurd. "In another world," he reflects, "circles, musical themes, keep their pure and rigid lines. . . . A circle is not absurd, it is clearly explained by the rotation of a segment of a straight line around one of its extremities. But neither does a circle exist."[9] The implication is that a circle, for example, as an almost Platonic entity, has no properties in excess of those it is defined as having (even if we only dimly perceive what all these properties are): all its properties are contained, as it were, in its concept, so that any characterization of a circle is, in Kant's terms, explicative rather than ampliative, a matter of analysis of what is already there in the understanding rather than an increment to our knowledge. So there are no conceptually superfluous properties here. To master the concept of the circle is to know all there is to know about circles. But real things, whose existence is external to any concept by means of which men may seek to cover them, will always have properties in excess of anything the concept may imply. "This root, by contrast, existed in such a way that I could not explain it." What does this mean, after all? Of course, one wants to object, we *can* explain roots, what they do and how they function. But this is not the sort of explanation that concerns and even obsesses Roquentin: *his* model of "explanation" is that of real definition and conceptual entailment, and while a real definition of "root" can be given, it will fail to individuate *this* root, and the definition would treat it as circles are treated, as though it contained nothing beyond what is given in the formula it indifferently shares with all members of the class of roots. "You could not pass from its function as a root, as a suction pump, to *that* [*a ça*], to that hard and thick hide of a sea lion, to

[9] *Ibid.*

this oily, callous, stubborn bark. The function explained nothing: it allowed you to understand in general what a root was, but not at all *that one there*."[10] Things are, and have to be, richer than any definition of them we might possibly frame, and indeed it would deflect entirely the point and purpose of definitions were we to seek one which perfectly individuated "that one there," a definition which not only was uniquely instantiated but which was as rich as the thing which instantiated it. Such a definition, were it possible, *would* be exactly as intelligible as the thing defined; it would duplicate in words the realities it was meant to apply to, and subvert the purposes of definition, if not of language, altogether. It would be something words could not do without losing that necessary abstractness which enables them to function descriptively: like the famous map spoken of by one of Lewis Carroll's characters, which just *was* the country, hill for hill, or an idle duplicate of it, which we would as much need a map to find our way around in as the country it iterated. Maps, and descriptions, have to differ from their subjects and must be general and abstract. But then, by a criterion which defines the posture of Roquentin/Sartre, and other mystics of language, they falsify: as though they could escape falsification only by being exactly what instead they merely represent. Language as language cannot, in this sense, but falsify.

Yet we cannot underestimate the extent of Sartre's futile passion to put the very concreteness of concrete things into words, words made equivalently concrete by the transformation, to *re*-produce the reality words ordinarily merely refer to—as though words were but, or could be but, the translation into a different medium

[10] *Ibid.*

*Absurdity: or, Language and Existence* | 15

of the "thereness" of persons and things, as though words could be made to stand to things as spoken words stand to written ones. Philosophy, as practiced before Sartre, was always as abstract as the linguistic medium it necessarily used, and it is just this that is implied in the quest for essences and definitions and conceptual liaisons, a kind of structural purity in which the tangled particularities of individual things are eliminated, and sometimes stigmatized as irrelevant or unintelligible— or even, in a sense not very remote from Sartre's, absurd. There was even a traditional question as to whether individuals were knowable as such at all. And Sartre was seeking a philosophy the reverse of this, and thought he had found it in phenomenology. Simone de Beauvoir, the companion of his life, tells of a marvelous encounter between him and Raymond Aron (this would have been in 1932):

> Raymond Aron was spending a year at the French institute in Berlin, and studying Husserl simultaneously with preparing an historical thesis. When he came to Paris he spoke of Husserl to Sartre. We spent an evening together at the Bec de Gaz in rue Montparnasse. We ordered the speciality of the house, apricot cocktails. Aron said, pointing to his glass: "You see, my dear fellow, if you were a phenomenologist, you could talk about this cocktail glass and make philosophy out of it." Sartre turned pale with emotion at this. Here was just the thing he had been longing to achieve for years—to describe objects just as he saw and touched them, and extract philosophy from the process.[11]

Phenomenology appeared to promise an escape from many things, not merely from generality but equally

[11] Simone de Beauvoir, *The Prime of Life*, trans. Peter Green, p. 112.

from that sort of preoccupation with subjectivity and the interior life to which the surrealists and the Freudians were at much the same time programmatically committed. In a kind of manifesto published in *La Nouvelle Revue Française* Sartre said: "We shall touch things themselves. We are no longer imprisoned in our sensations like Proustian men. Consciousness is always outside of itself, it is consciousness *of* something."[12] I shall defer to later chapters Sartre's theory of consciousness; it is the first sort of escape, from generality to concreteness, which interests me here, though the two preoccupations are closely linked throughout his philosophy. At the time of his encounter with Aron, he was already convinced, Simone de Beauvoir tells us, that "the world must be exactly as we perceive it to be, and that indeed nothing outside the domain of perceptibility is even intelligible"[13]—a kind of Berkeleyan view minus the idealistic implications for which Berkeley cherished it. "His aim," she writes, "was to preserve the phenomenon, the realities of the world. . . . One day I got him to defend the thesis that microbes and other animalculae invisible to the naked eye didn't exist at all. It was ridiculous, and he knew it, but he wouldn't climb down."

This narrowly empiricist criterion of reality has still to be distinguished from the obsession with individuating and totalizing descriptions, making them equivalent in specificity to the reality addressed. Nevertheless, the latter has been Sartre's theoretical aim throughout. It is exactly what he means, for instance, by existential psychoanalysis, whose goal is to show how "the in-

---

[12] Sartre, "Une idée fondamentale de la phénoménologie de Husserl," *La Nouvelle Revue Française*, no. 304 (January 1939), 131. Reprinted in *Situations, I* (Paris, 1947), pp. 34-35.
[13] Beauvoir, *op. cit.*, p. 39.

*Absurdity: or, Language and Existence* | 17

dividual [over] there" chose to live just the life he did live, that one and no other, and this specificity is not something which the generalized theoretical resources of standard psychoanalysis, or any science, can achieve. Varieties of men and women are indifferently victims of, say, the Oedipus complex, but to refer to this single explanatory concept is to treat them as *types* and to transcend the varieties of their responses and symptomologies. But this, again, is in his terms falsifying, even if it is no plainer that we can have a science which does not abstract than we can have a language which does not. Maximal individuation remains Sartre's ideal nevertheless, as though nothing else would preserve phenomena in their immediacy and uniqueness. It comes up again in his criticism of academicized Marxism in *Search for a Method*, for despite his expressed belief that Marxism is the sole philosophy viable for our age, the Marxist practice of explaining human behavior through reference to class affiliations of individual men, and then wiping out their individuality as though it were scientifically inscrutable, is once more falsifying and wrong. "Valéry was a petit-bourgeois intellectual," he writes in epitome of his argument, "but not every petit-bourgeois intellectual is a Valéry."[14] And the question is always to show how *this* man, *here*, Pascal or Baudelaire or Flaubert or Sartre himself, experienced and lived out his class identification in the manner in which he uniquely did; just as psychoanalysis has to be particularized existentially, so must Marxism be, and hence the latter requires existentialism if admittedly in a subordinate theoretical role. Sartre's latest major work, *L'Idiot de la famille* (1970), a four-volume study of Flaubert and *Madame Bovary*, is precisely this kind of

[14] *Search for a Method*, trans. Hazel Barnes, p. 56.

effort to explain and individuate at once, to show *this* life and why it was. Sartre is not just a man of words, as the title and chapter headings—"Reading" and "Writing"—of his singularly arch and moving autobiography confess. He has a magical view of what words can do, that they can slip the general character one would believe to be their essence and give us the substance of real things by some astounding literary transfiguration, almost as though words themselves were the "flesh of the world," to pre-empt and deliberately misapply a phrase of Maurice Merleau-Ponty.

Immediately after his meeting that evening with Aron, Sartre, who was himself to study the following year in Berlin, secured a volume on Husserl, and Simone de Beauvoir records his fear, in leafing through it, that his views on contingency might have been anticipated. He obviously considered them remarkably original. "To him," she writes, "general laws and concepts and all such abstractions were hot air: people, he maintained, all agreed to accept them because they effectively masked a reality which men found alarming. He, on the other hand, wished to grapple with the living reality and despised any analysis which limited its dissection to corpses."[15]

So Roquentin pretty much embodies Sartre's own view of this period, not only through his confrontation with the ineffabilities of the tree in the park, but later, in a remarkable meditation where, in addition to the radical contingency of existence as such, he perceives as a logical and hence vivid possibility that things should begin to behave in flagrant disconformity with the comfortable, shielding regularities which our general laws

[15] Beauvoir, *op. cit.*, p. 30.

## Absurdity: or, Language and Existence | 19

and, for that matter, our common sense imply we believe them constrained to follow.

> What if something were to happen? What if something suddenly started throbbing? Then they would notice it was there and they'd think their hearts were going to burst. Then what good would their dykes, boulevards, powerhouses, furnaces, and pile drivers be to them? It can happen any time, perhaps right now. For example, the father of a family might go for a walk and, across the street, he'll see something like a red rag, blown toward him by the wind. And when the rag has got close to him, he'll see that it is a side of rotten meat, grimy with dust, dragging itself along by crawling, skipping, a piece of writhing flesh rolling in the gutter, spasmodically shooting out spurts of blood. Or a mother might look at her child's cheek and ask him "What's that—a pimple?" and see the flesh puff out a little, split, open, and at the bottom of the split an eye, a laughing eye, might appear. Or they might feel things gently brushing against their bodies, like the caresses of reeds to swimmers in a river. And they will realize that their clothing has become living things. And someone else might feel something scratching in his mouth. He goes to the mirror, opening his mouth: and the tongue is an enormous, live centipede, rubbing its legs together and scraping his palate. He'd like to spit it out, but the centipede is part of him and he will have to tear it out with his own hands, And a crowd of things will appear for which people will have to find new names. . . .[16]

The passage goes on, a Boschian catalogue of appalling possibilities and an amazing example of a literary, not to say lurid, imagination at the service of a philosophical intuition. But the intuition is after all a familiar one,

---

[16] *Nausea*, pp. 212–13.

and essentially it is Hume's again, namely, that there is no necessity to our causal laws of the sort to be found in systems of logic or in analytical propositions; laws express what happen to be constant conjunctions of like events, and as a matter of abstract possibility the conjunctions could have been different or never constant. But, as is typical with Sartre, a philosophical thesis is transfigured into an existential fact. "Let it change," Roquentin says, "just a little, just to see, I don't ask for anything better."[17] The world is not governed by reason, and our view that it is ordered at all suitably to our purposes and survival is based on the most fragile luck, which could change any time.

But there is obviously more to this vehement passage than a surrealistic gloss on Hume: it breathes a deep hatred of *"them,"* who happen in the novel to be the bourgeois of Bouville, whose pompous portraits Roquentin saw hanging in the Municipal Museum. So it is an act of philosophical and artistic revenge against the smug and the comfortable assurance that there is an indelible, even benign order in the world in which "they" themselves—*"les Salauds!"*—participate and which underwrites their eminence as though it were a fact of nature, as though the universe meant them to have their property and position and security as a matter of natural necessity:

> Imbeciles . . . they make laws, they write popular novels, they get married, they are fools enough to have children. And all this time great, vague nature has slipped into the city . . . and they don't see it. They imagine it to be outside, twenty miles from the city. I *see* it. I *see* this nature. . . . I know that its obedience is idleness, I know it has no laws: what

[17] *Ibid.*, p. 218.

*Absurdity: or, Language and Existence* | 21

they take for constancy is only habits, and it can change tomorrow.[18]

And *when* it does—and note the shift from "if" to "when"—then, Roquentin says at the end of his extraordinary fantasy, he will *laugh*. "I'll lean against a wall and when they go by, I'll shout, "What's the matter with your science? What have you done with your humanism? Where is your dignity of the thinking reed?"[19] Sartre "rejected science," Simone de Beauvoir recalls, "but he went to unheard-of extremes in his rejection of universals."[20]

It is difficult to find another philosopher so nihilistically extreme, unless perhaps Nietzsche, whose view of nature was as unstructured and Dionysian, wildly different from any set of descriptions or beliefs, none of which are objectively validated and all of which are in principle false, except to the degree that they are convenient fictions enabling us to live a certain form of life. (The members of a given life-form are reinforced in their beliefs in virtue of being members of it, and this inertia is the enemy of other forms of life, equally possible if no more objectively valid.) But in the end it is not so much science, or even common sense, which Sartre rejects; not so much our beliefs about the world as our beliefs about these beliefs—our belief that they are true and correspond to an order antecedently there, transferring the logical ties of thought and language to nature, which in fact is wild. This propensity, and especially its extension to *moral* beliefs, Sartre speaks of as the spirit of "seriousness," and it is for their seriousness in this sense that he impugns the bourgeois men-

[18] *Ibid.*, p. 212.
[19] *Ibid.*, p. 213.
[20] Beauvoir, *op. cit.*, p. 30.

tality. It is notable that in describing his own character in *The Words*, Sartre speaks of his "lightness" or *légèreté*, an incapacity to take himself *au sérieux*: "Never in my life have I given an order without laughing."[21] And in the end the main charge against the bourgeoisie is less that they take nature seriously than that they take themselves that way. It can hardly be claimed, of course, that "seriousness" is a peculiarly bourgeois trait. It is, rather, a metaphysical attitude which must be evenly distributed across class lines. Men do not spontaneously distinguish their representations of the world from the way the world is—to believe that *p* is simply to believe that *p* is true—and it takes a special schooling in epistemology, or at least some rude conceptual shock, similar to if scarcely as dramatic as Roquentin appears to have sustained, to bring to consciousness the thought that there is a difference at all. We spontaneously refer our beliefs to the world, not so much as a matter of conscious philosophical doctrine but through the fact that we live in the world in a certain way and imply through our conduct that the world *is* the way in which we live it.

We shall return to the bourgeois of Bouville later, when we come to discuss Sartre's key notion of *mauvaise foi*—"bad faith"—which is, briefly, the view that we are what we are the way *things* or *objects* are what *they* are; that a man is a father or a waiter or a homosexual the way "an oak tree is an oak tree," instead of being radically free and inescapably contingent beings, creatures whose being is their freedom. Bad faith is wrong doctrine in Sartre's scheme, but once more it cannot be supposed a class doctrine of the bourgeoisie, though Sartre's hatred of his class is so profound that he is prepared

[21] *The Words*, trans. Bernard Frechtman, p. 21.

## Absurdity: or, Language and Existence | 23

to associate all bad philosophy with it and make a metaphysical scapegoat of it, so that society will be purified of all such errors when it is driven out at last. Sartre's attitude toward the bourgeoisie is chronic and negative, and was so well before any explicit endorsement on his part of Marxist or other political views. In the period of his life in which *Nausea* was written, for instance, he and Simone de Beauvoir held a largely neutral view on political questions: they were writers and intellectuals with no special commitments—or *engagements*, to use his characteristic phrase—at all. And this we shall see reflected in Roquentin's view of writing, which was pretty much Sartre's view at the time, before the dark experiences of World War II changed it radically, and he became, and urged all writers to become politically engaged. But even the notion of "engagement" is a technical concept, not merely an incendiary appeal.

In *Nausea*, which is a work of Sartre's philosophical youth, not even trees "are what they are." The chestnut tree is not "a chestnut tree" since the latter fails, like any nomic label, to capture the superabundant overflowing of the reality to which it is lamely applied. "I was the root of the chestnut tree,"[22] Roquentin cries at one point, in the empathic vernacular of the mystic, only to rephrase it in a moment: "or rather, I was entirely conscious of its existence. Still detached from it—since I was conscious of it—yet lost in it, nothing but it." And with this a note is sounded which is to dominate Sartre's philosophy throughout his life, for while Roquentin and the root have a common bond of contingency and *are* in a way more than can ever be said, the structures of a conscious being are going to differ from

[22] *Nausea*, p. 177.

those of the objects of consciousness, and a line is going to be drawn which prevents Roquentin or any of us from collapsing onto the objects of his or our consciousness, however much the latter (how metaphorically apt that the object here should be a *root*) should saturate one's consciousness of it. For there is no point at which one's awareness of the root will or can obliterate the further awareness that one is aware. And this line, in turn, will generate the whole of Sartre's metaphysics. However contingent the root may be, both in the sense that its existence is not given by its concept and in the further sense that its causal structures are never necessary and so it can and even might begin to behave differently, it can never be contingent in the way we are, for because it is a thing it is not conscious, and because it is not conscious it cannot be free. Freedom is *our* essence, in the respect that we *are* our freedom, and not something separate which just happens to have freedom but could lack this property or character. But this means that we have no essence in any further sense, there is nothing other than freedom which we are and which stains our nature from the start. Or: what we are is up to us to choose, except that we cannot *be* what we choose, only the act of choosing it. And this inalienable choice is never something Sartre is prepared to assign to trees, or to things, and the distinction between ourselves and mere inert objects becomes increasingly rigid as his philosophy evolves. Of course, because the distinction is Sartre's, drawing it right is going to be subtle and complex, and it will have to be delivered to the reader through the larger structures of Sartre's complete philosophy.

For Sartre's philosophy is a total, systematic edifice, however easily—because of his knack for epitomization—fragments of it can be detached and given cur-

## Absurdity: or, Language and Existence | 25

rency as slogans. "Existentialism," he says in his famous lecture on the subject, "is the least scandalous, the most austere of doctrines . . . intended strictly for specialists and philosophers."[23] And even the sloganized bits never quite mean within the system which generates them what they appear to mean to those to whom they appeal, any more with Sartre than with other vulgarly appealing but internally difficult thinkers like Nietzsche or Marx or Freud. Sartre defines existentialism sharply as the thought that "existence precedes essence,"[24] which he unhelpfully paraphrases as, "subjectivity must be the starting point." While this is true in a way, it is not true in one way in which it can be taken, for Sartre has no use for the interior life or its explorations, and in fact believes that there is no such thing *as* an interior life, everything being external to consciousness, something he tried to prove in his critique of Husserl. But in any case, that existence precedes essence has a fairly clear meaning in the case of human beings: they are not determined to be what they are through a fixed human nature in which they participate; it is their nature not to have a nature in this sense; and their lives are spent in quest of a self-definition which they cannot find in the terms in which they seek it. If they do find a definition, it will be a matter not of discovery but of decision: whatever we are is what we have decided to be, and we cannot therefore really *be* it since the option always is available to decide otherwise.

If Sartre has a central philosophical anthropology it is this, but I cite it here in order to stress that while it may explain what it means for *our* existence to precede our essence, no such explanation can be given of how

---

[23] *Existentialism*, trans. Bernard Frechtman, p. 15.
[24] *Ibid*.

this might apply to things. "Man is nothing else but what he makes of himself," Sartre writes, "this is the first principle of existentialism."[25] And this, we shall see, is a consequence of the way in which consciousness is structured, according to Sartre, which is what it is finally going to mean to say that "subjectivity is the starting point." "Man is at the start a plan which is aware of itself"—but, once more, nothing remotely like this can be true of things, as Sartre immediately goes on to say by distinguishing men as so characterized from "a patch of moss, a piece of garbage, or a cauliflower." So if existence precedes essence with things too, it must be for metaphysically different reasons. Perhaps, as Sartre appears to have believed from the beginning, there are no essences or universals at all, and what we take to be them are mere fictive contrivances of ours. Even so, the modes of being of things will remain totally unlike the mode of human existence, as much so as, in Berkeley's philosophy, minds or spirits exist different from things or ideas, and have virtually no common term with them. *They*, after all, are what they are, whereas, perplexing as it must sound at this stage of our exposition, just the opposite is true of us: we are what we are *not*, he will say in *Being and Nothingness*, and we are not what we are. So we will always be distinct from any characterization we may give of ourselves or may be given by others, and our greatest mistake—a mistake the extirpation of which it is Sartre's devoted mission to achieve—is to suppose that we are, or even that we are like such things as chestnut trees, with which Roquentin feels a momentary identification. It is impossible at this point to say more, either about things or ourselves, until we have revealed more philosophical

[25] *Ibid.*, p. 19.

## Absurdity: or, Language and Existence | 27

structure than the flashy inspirational invective that was all a popular lecture could afford.

Roquentin's shattering vision has few parallels or peers in literature, religious or secular. It bears comparison in its integrity, scope, and totality to the revelation of his nature with which Krishna graces Arjuna at the climax of the *Gita*, or with which the Erdgeist demoralizes Faust. It is unlikely that a man can undergo such an experience and emerge unaltered, for it calls into question the defining framework of his heretofore uncriticized existence, an existence whose inadequacy was prefigured viscerally by the nausea which the vision now explains. One could respond to such an experience by insanity or suicide or by religiously revolutionizing one's life, or one could emerge so broken spiritually that the concept of a meaningful existence would have gone unendurably hollow. It is not in the nature of the existentialist hero to be destroyed by such revelations, however. Rather, once the condition of his being is shown to him, he sets forth to change his life, or better, to change the kind of life he henceforth is to live in the light of the new and previously unimaginable knowledge. Heidegger speaks, for instance, of an *authentic* existence, which becomes available just when men internalize the thought of death, when they realize not just that all men are mortal, which everyone appreciates, but that *they* have to die their *own* deaths and that no one else can do it for them, and so then can be liberated to live their own lives—not as "one" but as themselves. Sartre's major novel, *Roads to Liberty*, is a study in the morphology of authenticity in this sense, of how quite different sorts of men arrive at an internal understanding of their own freedom, and hence of their ultimate responsibility, which is solely theirs and cannot be shrugged off onto politics or sexuality or whatever, an understanding which they had all along but which they concealed from themselves through various mechanisms of bad faith that become, at a certain point, transparent to the victim.

In *Nausea* Roquentin resolves to write a novel, a bid for redemption from inauthenticity which by itself merits a few comments. The exaltation of art has always played a part in postromantic consciousness, but Roquentin's decision is predictably a philosophical one, and it presupposes a thesis in the ontology of art without which it must seem singularly tepid and disproportionate to the experience to which it responds. And it is a decision which demands for its appreciation the apparatus of essence and existence. Works of art are *not* superfluous, as it turns out, because in a sense they do not exist, and so they promise an escape from superfluousness and contingency.

Roquentin arrives at this conception of a work of art while hearing for a last time a favorite record in a café before quitting the city of mud. (The number of philosophical discoveries made in a café in Sartre's work are equaled at best by the number of them made in parks, and one regrets for more than the obvious reasons the absence of that genial institution in the English-speaking world.) The voice of a black woman sings "Some of These Days." The record, as it happens, is scratched. But the *song* is not scratched. The song cannot be affected by the accidental modification of the crass vehicle through which it is communicated. I can burn the book in which a poem is printed, but the poem as such is logically uninflammable. "Behind the existent which tumbles from one moment to another, without past, without future, behind these sounds which decompose from day to day, are chipped away and slide toward death, the melody remains the same, young and

## Absurdity: or, Language and Existence | 29

steady, like a witness without pity." Roquentin romanticizes the composer who wrote the cheap song and the black woman who sings it, and concludes that through the shallow, jaunty tune they somehow have been saved, their existences somehow justified, for they have produced something beyond existence. Roquentin will himself be saved and justified if he can bring his novel off: "behind the printed words, behind the pages, something which did not exist, which would be above existence."[26] *Then*, Roquentin supposes, he might be able to accept himself. Artworks, on this view, stand outside reality, like Platonic forms. "Some of These Days," in this regard, is like Keats's Grecian urn, a thing of beauty and a joy forever because whatever might happen to it nothing can happen to the figures it shows, logically frozen as they are in the postures and gestures given them by the artist; they remain eternally young and perpetually loving. And Sartre's conception of the artist himself at this time is like that of Yeats in "Sailing to Byzantium," who seeks to flee contingency by transforming himself into something outside nature: "Once out of nature I shall never take/ My bodily form from any natural thing,/But such a form as Grecian goldsmiths make/ of hammered gold and gold enamelling . . ."

There is unquestionably a certain truth in this: I can touch the marble, but David is intangible; I can hear the actor but never Romeo—Juliet alone hears *him*; I can see the paint but not the nympheas, which are in a space of their own, discontinuous with my optical space. "A painting," Sartre wrote in one of his studies on the imagination, "cannot be illuminated by projecting a beam of light on the canvas: it is the canvas that is

[26] *Nausea*, pp. 234–35, 237.

illuminated, not the painting."[27] But, we might point out, much the same thing can be said regarding the differences between sentences and the propositions they express. A sentence can be illuminated but its meaning remain as dark as I found it, and the meaning of a sentence printed long ago can undergo changes without these being reflected in the instant inky chemistry of the printed line. What Sartre celebrates so portentously here may just be the difference between a plain mark and a meaningful one, and it is not clear that we are dealing so much with two orders of reality complexly interconnected, like Platonic forms and their appearances in the sublunar world, as we are with the admittedly interesting distinction between a thing and a rule for its interpretation. But Sartre insists that artworks enjoy a specially privileged sort of reality, and there is certainly a sense in which a parallel can be drawn between them and the circles Roquentin reflected on. For artworks are fully determinate in the sense that there are certain questions one cannot ask about their contents. The house of Proust's aunt in Illiers had a certain number of steps, and they could be counted by a visitor, but the stairs in Tante Léonie's house in Combray have no determinate number, nor is there any way of knowing how many steps there are; such questions cannot be answered or seriously raised within the boundaries of the novel. So it is not like the root, which always contains answers to any question about it we may pose. We shall never recover a determinate biology of dragons from a scrutiny however sustained of *Beowulf*'s depiction of Grendel; all there is to know is there, and Grendel has no existence outside his

---

[27] *The Psychology of the Imagination*, trans. Bernard Frechtman, p. 212.

depiction. In any case, it is as though an artwork were like the intersection of two worlds, one of which we occupy and one of which we cannot, and the work itself is *in* but not *of* the world to which *we* are subject.

This hyperaesthetic, precious view of art and artistic creativity sounds, and is, extremely remote from the view we have generally come to identify as Sartre's, of literature as "engaged" and artists as "committed," as disclosing reality rather than building an alternative one, the point being not to stand outside the world but to change it. As a matter of ontology, perhaps, his view of artworks might guardedly be accepted, but his view of the act and point of writing evidently changed by the time he came to write his essay *What is Literature?* Language used for literary and, in the final redemptive pages of *Nausea*, for transfigurative and salvational ends falls roughly under the rubric of poetry, in terms of the distinctions framed in *What is Literature?*, in the sense that its product is a kind of word-thing, where the words themselves, as it were, are the objects in which the artistic act results; in the generalized sense that we may think of things as opaque, existing in themselves, and without ulterior references, poetry is opaque. To be sure, words melded into a word-thing do not quite lose their significance as words. They are not just noises. But, in the poetic attitude, we remain concerned with words as words, rather than with what, in the context of prose or ordinary discourse, the words are about or to what they usually refer. A poet may express emotion, but when he does so, the emotion is put into the words: the words *are* the emotion metamorphosed: they are thus not *about* the emotion they express. And this may be supposed generally to be the case with words employed poetically: they metamorphose reality rather than designate it and so are, in a way, fragments of reality given verbal embodiment. This is the ideal of language as such as construed in *Nausea*. There is, as with metamorphosis generally, something of a magical order here: poems *are* things rather than about things, even if they are made of words; and the poet is a kind of transformer or maker, as the concept of *poesis* etymologically recommends. In prose, by contrast, words are used transparently, transporting us to a reality beyond themselves, and we recognize them as having no substance of their own to arrest the understanding. There is, Sartre supposes—like Monsieur Jourdain—nothing in common between poetry and prose so conceived; they are, to use a distinction familiar to logicians, as disparate as the use and the mention of a term. The difference in function between prose and poetry in the literary act comes to this: poets use words in just the wrong way for poets to be "engaged," whereas the prose writer uses them in such a way that he cannot *but* be engaged. Instead of putting things into words, he *uses* words, as speakers do, and does something by means of them: "he designates, demonstrates, orders, refutes, interprets, begs, insults, persuades, insinuates."[28] In prose, words are actions rather than things.

Since J. L. Austin, at least, a conception of language as performative has been a dominating idea in Anglo-Saxon linguistic philosophy. It was Austin's criticism of many, perhaps most philosophical treatments of language that they took language primarily as descriptive, primarily through its capacity to state truths; and while, undoubtedly, it has this function, it is not an exclusive or even, Austin implied, a primary function; to suppose otherwise is to have committed what he dubbed the De-

[28] Sartre, *What is Literature?*, trans. Bernard Frechtman, pp. 13–14.

scriptive Fallacy. His most famous contribution lay in showing (or at least in suggesting) that many central philosophical phrases were in fact performative rather than descriptive; that when, for instance I say that I *know* something, I am not describing a fact about myself, am not reporting a cognitive achievement (which may then give rise to questions of what cognitive achievements are), but rather, I am giving my word to my communicant, as much so as if I say to him that I promise thus and such. Sartre's theory, less astutely phrased, is similar to this. But even with description, Sartre says, I am after all *doing* something: it is an error "to think that the word is a gentle breeze which plays lightly over the surfaces of things, which grazes them without altering them, and that the speaker is a pure witness who sums up with a word his harmless contemplation."[29] No. "To speak is to act, anything which we name is no longer quite the same: it has lost its innocence." To pronounce the word "thief" in the presence of a thief is not merely to imply that the individual so designated is so called: "if you name the behavior of an individual, you reveal it to him; he sees himself." The function of naming in this way is to bring to the consciousness of the nominee what he really is—if the target of a name is to begin with capable of conscious self-representation: it is less obvious that we alter the state of a fish by giving it its name—or at least another theory of how we do so is required. In the case of men, to describe them is to show them to themselves as they are shown to us, so that they come not only—and the complications here are typically Sartrian, and will play a role in the economy of man's relations with others as he diagnoses them in *Being and Nothingness*

[29] *Ibid.*, p. 16.

—to know themselves but to know that others know them this way: and this cannot but (Sartre supposes) induce modification in their behavior. Calling the young Genet a thief, for instance, not merely identified him as having stolen, but gave him, according to Sartre's treatment, an identity and a project: it caused him to *be* a thief, since it was through the network of associations with this term that he henceforth saw himself; and as he believed himself to be, so did he act, and the power of the name consisted in causing the fact it did not neutrally merely designate.[30]

So description does not contrast with linguistic performance: it is "action by disclosure," and even if Sartre's theory has primary or exclusive application when the subjects of discourse are human and alive, it would be a mistake to suppose that the descriptive function is invariantly the same whether the subjects be human or mere things. In any event, since to speak is to act, to speak discursively is *ipso facto* to be engaged, and the question then always can be raised as to what one means to be doing when one speaks, what aspect of the world one means to open up through speaking of it, language opening up the world in much the way, we shall see, that consciousness does. And to reveal is to change, if only to the extent that revelation itself is a change, so there is in effect no ideal nonpoetic use of language, only perhaps ineffective uses; and no description is impartial, no speaker godlike and detached, set over and against an external reality simply there to be encoded. Even *silence* can be a form of speech, revelation, and action in a degenerate sense. The writer is always exposed to the query, "Why have you spoken of this

[30] *Saint Genet, Actor and Martyr*, trans. Bernard Frechtman, *passim*.

*Absurdity: or, Language and Existence* | 35

rather than that, and—since you speak in order to bring about change—why do you want to change this rather than that?"[31] Writing is *choice*. Of course, if writing is and cannot but be engaged, the force of an appeal to writers to become engaged loses its point, since they already are. But, here as elsewhere, *calling* what they do "engagement" is to reveal the character of their action to them, and more than this Sartre does not want.

Sartre draws a crucial distinction between reading and writing, and it runs very deep indeed. Suppose a writer is stuck and does not know what to do next, how to go on. This is very different from a reader who does not know what is coming next. And the point is available throughout the domain of action—between actors and witnesses of acts, between, for example (Sartre uses this one in his early book on the emotions), observing myself drawing a line and observing someone else doing so: *I* know what I am doing in a way in which I don't know what another is doing, or another me.[32] The writer makes the words, he does not read them; reading calls for a wholly different attitude and position of knowledge with regard to the words. So the writer cannot write for himself. He requires a reader, and he writes for him. Literature demands "the conjoint effort of author and reader. . . . There is no art except for and by others."[33]

That reading is a creative act and conceptually entailed by the concept of writing—which is after all more than making marks on a surface—is a striking but not an especially novel thought. What *is* novel in Sartre

---

[31] *What is Literature?*, p. 19.
[32] Sartre, *The Emotions: Outline of a Theory*, trans. Bernard Frechtman, p. 45.
[33] *What is Literature?*, p. 37.

is the thought that reading is an essentially free act, not merely a response to some words but the constitution of an object—the *work*—which does not exist anterior to its constitution and is not identical with the words, which cannot *cause* the act of reading. The appearance of the work is a "new event which cannot be explained by anterior data." Writing presupposes the freedom of readers to constitute works which would be only words without them. But so is writing itself free, for since distinct from the words themselves, neither work nor words can cause one another. In a typical sort of phrase, Sartre says: "The work of art, from whatever side you approach it, is an act of confidence in the freedom of men." But indeed, all literature is this. "Thus whether he is an essayist, a pamphleteer, a satirist, or a novelist, whether he speaks only of individual passions or whether he attacks the social order, the writer, a free man addressing free men, has only a single subject—freedom."[34]

One feels that something very odd has taken place by the time one reaches this ringing, edifying conclusion. It may indeed be true that neither reading nor writing can be caused by works to whose constitution they are instead essential. We may cautiously agree that reading and writing are free actions as far as reference to the work, as their common effect, is concerned. But whether in any larger or absolute sense they are free and novel has to be grounded in some more profound analysis. Equally, even if it is true that the artwork requires two collateral interlocking freedoms in order to exist at all, it will not follow that freedom is the *subject* of all writing, or all art, any more than it follows from the fact

[34] *Ibid.*, pp. 40, 57, 58.

that writing demands a medium and a surface that the *subject* of all writing is inscription.

On the other hand, it has almost always been true of Sartre, since *Nausea*, that *his* subject is freedom. This is certainly so in his novel *Roads to Liberty*; it has been true in his political and psychological writings and in his biographical and critical writings as well: exactly the *choice* by which Baudelaire and Genet and Flaubert framed the lives they lived is the subject of his studies. Freedom is almost vulgarly the subject of *The Flies*, a play of 1942, and its absence among the effectively dead is the more sophisticated subject of *No Exit*. The concept of choice, at times agonized choice, is the animating theme of Sartre's dramatic literature generally. But it is in his major philosophical work, his masterpiece, *Being and Nothingness*, that we encounter its most serious thematic development and the most rigorous, least rhetorical and stylized of Sartre's various discussions of it. It is accordingly to this deep, intricate logical labyrinth, with its astonishing ontology and human insights, that we must turn to appreciate what freedom means for Sartre.

## Nothingness: or, Consciousness and Ontology

## ii

The subtitle of *Being and Nothingness* is *An Essay in Phenomenological Ontology*. Commentators have supposed this to be a contradiction of sorts, inasmuch as phenomenology is the study of the way things appear to consciousness without reference to questions of truth or falsity, illusion or reality, or whether these are appearances of existing things or not; whereas ontology is concerned with what there is, a philosopher's ontology consisting in his catalogue of the logically distinct orders of things he believes the universe to be made up of. One *can* say that the universe consists solely of what appears to consciousness, but this is already to advance a proposition beyond what phenomenology ought to allow, it being merely concerned with appearances without regard to their status, with the content of appearance, as it were. So how shall

## Nothingness: or, Consciousness and Ontology | 39

phenomenology and ontology be compatible philosophical enterprises?

As it happens, the conflict arises from a shallow conception of each. To begin with, the phenomenologist is not a mere descriptive recorder of phenomena as experienced; he is, rather, interested in the *structures* of the phenomenological field and with the most general sorts of principles spontaneously employed in the organization of experience. Thus it is of concern to him whether time is something we experience or whether it is instead a way in which experiences are ordered, and he shelves as irrelevant to these inquiries such questions as may arise in connection with time as a physical parameter, say. The phenomenologist, then, is to be interested in just the sorts of concepts which philosophers always have been—causality and existence, appearance and reality, identity and difference—but he attempts to get at these through discovering the functions they serve in the structures of experiences. In this sense he is carrying forward a program initiated by Kant in the first great division of the *Critique of Pure Reason*.

Ontology, on the other hand, is not simply a *catalogue raisonné* of the kinds of entities which make up the universe; the ontologist is not just a maker of abstract lists; nor could one build up much of an ontology by roaming the world with pencil in hand, making note of what one encountered (dishes, dogs, ducks, dyspeptic draughtsmen) with a negative ontology of the unencountered (deities, dodos, dragons), to follow the alphabetical orientation of the Autodidact. For most of the items in respectable ontologies are not ordinarily encounterable: or the class of encounterables may constitute just one ontological order, and the serious question would be how many, if any, other distinct orders there were. But this question arises only relative to a particular discourse, and concerns the entities we are *required* to countenance on the assumption that this discourse is true. Thus, whether or not there are electrons is by itself an idle wonder, and the issue rather is whether we are committed in some way to assume their existence, and this is a matter of whether a theory in which the term "electron" functions referentially is true. Plato's ontology included numbers, and Pythagoras's ontology included nothing else, but whether they were right is more or less a matter of faith, the deep question being whether the truth of mathematical propositions commits us to such entities. If, for example, mathematics can be reduced to arithmetic and arithmetic to set-theory, then all we are required to admit into our ontology will be sets. The obligation imposed upon philosophers is to seek an account of the whole of reality, and it is a matter of intellectual responsibility to base this on the narrowest ontology one can get by with. Bertrand Russell, for example, believed that sentences ostensibly about physical objects could be shown to be analyzable finally as sentences about sense-data—physical objects were "logically constructed" out of these—and though there may indeed be more on earth and in heaven than sense-data, Russell at least believed that he had no *commitment* to anything beyond these, and that in terms of them he could finally account for whatever had to be accounted for. So the problems of ontology cannot easily be isolated from considerations concerning language, meaning, and truth.

Thus the extreme importance of definition in philosophy, which has nothing to do with lexicography as such. To be able to define one set of terms by means of another is to be able to that extent to reduce our ontological commitments, and when this proves impos-

## Nothingness: or, Consciousness and Ontology | 41

sible for certain terms, they must be reckoned primitive and their designata irreducible items in our ontological scheme. Thus have philosophers thought that, in addition to encounterable things like material objects and perhaps persons, there must be such things as universals, Platonic forms, substances, properties, facts of various orders (positive and negative, singular and general), and a variety of other odd entities—less as monstrous posits of the untethered speculative intellect, which ontologists would jettison if they could, than as objects which seemed, for whatever reason, uneliminable if discourse were to be applied.

It is now simple enough to descry the connection between ontology and phenomenology in the Sartrian scheme. Phenomenology is concerned, as we saw, with the structures of consciousness, and ontology concerns the sorts of beings that such structures must commit us to on the assumption that this analysis is "true." So the question again is not what there is, but what we are constrained to suppose there is with reference to the structures we have determined as belonging to consciousness. Sartre believed, in a way, that there is no difference to be marked here at all, that the world is just the way it is revealed through the structures of consciousness to be; and a kind of argument can be mounted in support of this view—it will imply that we cannot intelligibly raise questions about reality save as it is given to us, since consciousness's limits are just the limits of intelligibility. Merleau-Ponty used such an argument, as did Berkeley before him, and Sartre too assumed something like it. In any case, he proposes that the analysis of the structures of consciousness yields two ontologically primitive types of being: conscious beings, which he terms *êtres-pour-soi*, or beings-for-themselves, beings part of whose nature is that they are aware of themselves and cannot exist as such without this awareness; and *êtres-en-soi*, beings which exist in themselves and are objects for an alien consciousness, having no consciousness of their own. The terms are borrowed from Hegel's *für-sich* and *an-sich*—they would have been too well known to be stolen—and one of Sartre's claims is that nothing can be, or have, both sorts of being at once: nothing can be *pour-et-en-soi* (though this would be just the structure of God, and will also be the impossible sort of being to which the *pour-soi* unremittingly aspires). A third type of being figures prominently in the latter parts of *Being and Nothingness*, namely *être-pour-autrui*, or being-for-others, and the *pour-soi* can, as it happens to his torment, have this third sort of being. Importantly, so can the *en-soi*, though Sartre makes little of this, at least explicitly—but, as we will see in chapter iii, it is an extremely important ontological category for him. Beings *en-soi* are just that: they exist in themselves, at least in the respect that their existence does not depend on anyone's consciousness of them; this is patently not the case for the *pour-soi*, which also, as we shall see, logically depends upon something other than itself, namely, upon those things other than itself of which it is conscious.

These are all types or modes of Being, and so none of them falls within the reference of Nothingness, and Nothingness is not, in this sense, quite an ontological category. Nevertheless, nothingness is a concept Sartre obviously feels it to be of great importance to get clear, and he is going to show that it is related in an intimate way to the *pour-soi*. He does say such things as this: the *pour-soi* is its own nothingness, and is that through which nothingness enters into our representation of the world. But even so, the *pour-soi* is not a non-entity, inasmuch as conscious being is a *kind* of being. We must allow all these intricately interconnected divisions to emerge gradually, along with the larger philosophical structures from which they derive their conceptual contours: as elsewhere, which is the despair of Sartre's expositors, everything has somehow to be given at once. We are dealing with a piece of ambitious metaphysical architecture, not just an odd list of what there is.

The primary structure of consciousness, the absolute beginning point, as much for Sartre as for the entire phenomenological school, is that consciousness always is *of* something. It is not, so to speak, a pure state, and no one is merely conscious without there being something of which he is conscious. I suppose a question might come up when we speak of someone regaining consciousness, after a faint or upon waking up, but even so, restoration of consciousness would not be like restoration of heartbeat: to be conscious is to be aware in a transitive way of something external to consciousness; consciousness will always have some content, however dimly and confusedly presented. And this is so for psychological states generally—memory and desire, hope and belief, anger and love: there is always an object for these in some sense of the term. It makes no sense, for example, to speak of *merely* believing: one must believe something or other to be the case; one loves something or someone, is angry at this or that, and so on. This inexpugnable feature of *aboutness*—or intensionality, to introduce the technical term—is what makes the basic difference between conscious beings and mere things, between Roquentin and the root of the chestnut tree, which may totally occupy his consciousness as an object without the distinction between his consciousness and its object being thereby obliterated.

Intensionality has come under intensive philosophical

investigation in recent times, as much by logicians as by phenomenologists, and it is now widely acknowledged that propositions attributing psychological properties to individuals—like "Sartre believes (or hopes, or fears, or desires, or even is nauseated) that $p$"—have interestingly different logical properties than those used to describe objects uncomplicated by the structures of consciousness or mentality. Thus, if a man $m$ believes that something $a$ has property F, it will not automatically follow that he believes that $b$ has property F, even if $a$ and $b$ are identical. But it is a logical truth that if $a$ and $b$ are identical, then $b$ is F if $a$ is F, whatever F may be. So we may substitute $a$ and $b$ for one another without altering the truth-value of the sentence in which the substitution is made—*unless* the sentence is a psychological one, so to speak. For it may be false that Sartre is nauseated that $a$ is F, even if it is true that Sartre is nauseated that $b$ is F and $a$ and $b$ are one and the same. Why there is this difference I shall not here try to say, nor shall I cite other differences between these two sorts of sentences, but it may be noted in passing that the term "nausea" in my example is used as a psychological predicate rather than a physiological one, nausea as a state of consciousness having an object and nausea as a mere physiological malaise having none. Or better, nausea as a mode of consciousness has an object as well as a cause, whereas nausea as a state, say, of the gut, has only a cause. Too many pickles may cause nausea, but the nausea is not *about* those pickles, and indeed not about anything. But nausea, as a Sartrian category, is quite definitely *about* something, and so stands as an intensional concept. But let us address ourselves for the moment to intensional objects, or the objects of consciousness.

It is somewhat delicate to move from examples like

## Nothingness: or, Consciousness and Ontology | 45

belief, whose object—*what* one believes—may be expressed by means of a proposition, to mere awareness, whose objects cannot always be thus expressed. Because he was mainly concerned with awareness, Sartre was not as sensitive as he might have been to the sorts of logical differences I alluded to above: his concern was less with peculiarities in the logic of psychological discourse than with what he thought of as ontological peculiarities arising from the structures of awareness. When he speaks of consciousness's objects, he tends to talk of things *sans façon*—of apples or traffic on the boulevard Saint-Germain, rather than of the apple being red or the traffic heavy—so he is concerned always, as we may put it, with consciousness *of* rather than consciousness *that*, and with objects of consciousness expressed by means of simple accusatives instead of propositions. This makes a greater difference than the unphilosophical reader might appreciate, for it conceals some important structures which are germane to his problems.

It is quite crucial in working out Sartre's philosophy to recognize from the start that he believes that the objects of which we are consciously aware are real objects: bits of the real world. This is not beyond controversy, for Descartes also believed consciousness—or "thought"—to be intensional (speaking anachronistically, since the term was not in Descartes's vocabulary), but he supposed the objects of consciousness always to be our own ideas—the contents of our minds—which we then believe, truly or falsely, to represent correspondent, external things. But Sartre supposes that we are directly aware of what Descartes believed we can know only through the mediation of ideas; even in the case of imagination, for Sartre we are aware not of imaginary objects but of real things, so that even if in imagination it is true to speak of someone having an image, the image is not the object of imagination, which is instead a *way* of being related to the real world.[1]

It has been a benchmark of philosophical thought since Plato to distinguish appearances from reality, a distinction which was given a special formulation in the writing of Kant, according to whom all we ever do experience are appearances—or phenomena—and never things in themselves, or *an-sich*—as though the objects of experience were an opaque film through which we cannot gain access to the world out there. So the Sartrian claim that objects of consciousness are things in themselves—*en-soi*—has a polemical connotation to the initiate. In general, post-Kantian philosophy in Europe and elsewhere may be said to consist in the effort to obliterate the gap between things and their appearances. A collective, massive attack on the dangling *Ding-an-sich* was mounted by Hegel and later by Husserl, reminiscent in a way of Berkeley's celebrated attack on the concept of material substrate—that colorless and odorless "I know not what" which allegedly underlay the qualities of experienced things and to which Berkeley could attach neither sense nor need. The upshot was that appearances and reality were one, that behind things as they appeared there was nothing we need reckon in our ontologies. The *Ding-an-sich* could be amputated from our scheme without the slightest tremor being felt, so there need not be an ulterior reality with which invidiously to contrast appearances. In a way, when the contrast goes, so does the characterization of one term: the very concept of appearance, at least in the sense of its being counterposed to reality, ought to have lost currency altogether. That it retained some

[1] Sartre, *The Psychology of the Imagination*, p. 11.

## Nothingness: or, Consciousness and Ontology | 47

meaning was because post-Kantian philosophers spoke of appearances less with reference to what they would be *of*, than with reference to the fact that appearances must be *to* something, namely to a consciousness, it being the other side of the concept that there is no consciousness save of something, that there are no appearances save to some consciousness. And this gives rise to the problem with which *Being and Nothingness* begins its argument.

If things are just appearances-to, then the world as made up of appearances must logically depend upon someone's being conscious of it, which is the consequence the idealist Berkeley was delighted to draw. But this is repugnant to the realistic prejudices of common sense, according to which things exist independently of our or anyone's consciousness of them; that there was a world before anyone was aware that there was; and that things are not somehow annihilated the moment they fall outside the range of awareness. Realism so construed is exactly Sartre's philosophy, and it was therefore imperative that he solve the problem of appearance in order to save his view that we are conscious of real, independent things. His analysis is striking and ingenious. I shall paraphrase it as follows: To believe that one is in the presence of a real object—say an apple—is to believe that it has aspects other than those of which one is directly aware at the moment; if the belief is true, the apple has aspects not given to consciousness when *it* is given to consciousness. Individual appearances, on the other hand, do not have aspects— they *are* aspects—but if it is an appearance of a thing, it belongs to something whose aspects are not exhausted by the appearance itself; there is no limit to the number of further, different appearances the thing might in principle reveal. The number is infinite, loosely speaking, or at least indeterminate. So to refer to an appearance as a *thing* is implicitly to refer to the multiplicity of the thing's appearances, and to believe in the reality of what one is aware of is to believe in a series of appearances to which the immediate appearance belongs. The infinite remainder of the series is thus just that inexhaustibility of which Roquentin had a vision when he encountered reality in the park of Bouville, as well as of his recognition that things—the famous root—are never totally given at once or through any finite set of revealed properties.

We left unanswered, in our discussion of *Nausea*, the *meaning* of "existence," and now we are in position to clarify it. Existence is not a property of things—"existence" is not a predicate, as Kant said—but, rather, is the fact that an appearance belongs to a series. So, to say that something exists is to say that there is more to it than one is aware of at the time, or can be at any time. Existence is simply the principle of the series, not a member of it. In a way, existence itself does not appear, which is why the vision in *Nausea* is rather of a mystical order. "But being is neither one of the object's qualities, capable of being apprehended among others, nor a meaning of the object. The object does not refer to being as a signification."[2] Existence nevertheless may form part of the content of a judgment to the effect that the appearance before us belongs to something which has appearances beyond the given one. And so to affirm reality is to affirm an independence of consciousness, which will mean, as the concept of consciousness

---

[2] *Being and Nothingness*, trans. Hazel Barnes, p. xlix. I have pretty much followed Dr. Barnes's felicitous translations throughout. The reader equipped with French can locate the relevant passage in *L'Être et le néant* (Paris, 1943) without difficulty.

## Nothingness: or, Consciousness and Ontology | 49

is developed, an independence of one's freedom. That is, it may be up to me what further experiences I shall seek, but not up to me what further experiences I shall find: "the series of its appearances is bound by a principle which does not depend on my whim."[3] This, we may observe, is a traditional criterion of reality, to be found alike in Descartes and in Locke, that what is real does not depend upon the will, even if what is there and what I would will to be there happen to coincide. And by these arguments Sartre hopes to have vindicated his claim that the objects of consciousness are real.

The degree to which he succeeds in any given case depends, of course, upon whether the belief in there being appearances beyond the appearance of the moment is true. And certainly there is no way in which one can know that it is true on the basis of the appearances at hand. Sartre admits as much when he says that the object, or series, is wholly within, and wholly outside,[4] a given appearance. It is wholly within to the extent that we believe the latter to belong *to* a series. It is wholly outside, for the series itself will never appear nor can it appear. But we could be wrong in every instance without its following that Sartre has not given a correct analysis of the concept of reality, meaning having to be distinguished here as elsewhere from knowledge, and conceptual analysis from epistemological truth. Nevertheless there is a problem here. Suppose in a given instance the belief *is* false, and the appearance does not belong in the series we supposed it had when we attributed reality to what we had experienced: what is the status of the appearance then? What is the object of awareness in this case? Philosophers

[3] *Ibid.*, p. xlvii.
[4] *Ibid.*

will recognize here a crux, out of which the entire structure of classical epistemology can be generated, since some objects of consciousness might not be real in the required sense, and in the extreme case none of them may be. It is just here that the specter of skepticism and the Problem of the External World rise to threaten us. I will not respond to the threat, save to acknowledge its inescapability even for Sartrian analysis. But I shall underscore that what he succeeded in doing is less to establish the reality of consciousness's objects than to articulate the concept of what it means to judge something real. Perhaps he has a pragmatic argument as well, namely, that to experience something is spontaneously to believe it to belong to a series whose further components are beyond our immediate awareness. But nothing in the content of what I experience supports or can support this belief, which may be false even if inevitable. What Sartre has done has been to establish a structure of consciousness, to analyze the notion of objective reality, and to identify what must be the case if the structure has application. Hence he will at once have done a piece of phenomenological analysis and have identified a piece of spontaneous ontology. The argument yields, at most, some clarity on what we must believe we are conscious of when we believe we are conscious of reality. To be sure, he has in a way done more than this. He has shown that things can be analyzed as the sum of their appearances, a point which acquires a special relevance when applied to men: the artist is the sum of his works, Sartre is what Sartre has done, one is the set of one's actions. To dissociate myself from the trail of products in which my history consists, to insist that I am not (merely) them, is going to be a possibility—providing (odd as this may sound) that I am alive. This will prove a torment to Garcin, the male character in *No Exit*, as well as to his female hell-mates. But this takes us considerably ahead of our account.

It will be useful at this point to introduce a somewhat technical term. The thing *transcends* any of its appearances, even if it cannot transcend, because it *is*, the total series of them (if we can speak of a closed totality here). So, in at least the favorable case, the phenomenon—what appears—is presupposed as having a transphenomenal foundation and consequently "surpasses the knowledge which we have of it and provides the basis for such knowledge."[5] And transcendence then minimally implies independence of consciousness. But what of the being of consciousness itself? And what of our knowledge not of the objects of consciousness but of our consciousness itself? Is, for instance, consciousness ever an object for itself, the way a table or an apple might be an object for it? If so, then by the arguments just rehearsed, we would have to treat consciousness as a being *en-soi*, a thing amongst things, and so transcendent and independent of itself, which sounds absurd, as well as inconsistent with the enterprise of wanting to distinguish consciousness of things from the things of consciousness.

So let us concentrate now on another structure of consciousness. To be conscious, we should recall, is to be conscious of something which, we now see, is believed to be independent of consciousness itself. Suppose we speak of knowledge here—or of "knowing consciousness," as Sartre describes it: of knowing something is a table because one is conscious of a table one believes to be there. Then, Sartre says, a necessary and sufficient condition for consciousness to be knowl-

[5] *Ibid.*, p. 1.

edge in this sense is that "it be consciousness of itself as being that knowledge."[6] Briefly, to know $x$ is to know that one knows $x$: to be aware is to be aware of being aware. Sartre says that this is a necessary and not merely a sufficient condition. One may agree that it is a sufficient condition: obviously, to know that one knows that $p$, is to know that $p$. One can't know what is not the case. Most epistemologists will concur. But that we have a *necessary* condition is immeasurably more debatable. Can one really say that I cannot know at all unless I know that I know? Some philosophers have supposed as much. Spinoza did so, for instance, and so did the British philosopher H. A. Prichard, and the contemporary Scandinavian thinker Jaakko Hintikka believes something quite close to this.[7]

Sartre offers only one, very condensed argument in support of his claim: a consciousness which is not simultaneously a consciousness of itself would be an *unconscious*—and this he feels is absurd, perhaps because he thinks "unconscious" just means "not conscious," and of course it would be absurd to suppose something might be at once a consciousness and not a consciousness. But the argument is exceedingly poor and overlooks the essential point about consciousness, namely, that it always is about something. Suppose, then, that I were conscious of something without being conscious of being so. I might be conscious (of an apple) and unconscious (of being conscious of the apple) at the same time, and there is nothing absurd about this; it does not entail that *consciousness* itself is unconscious. Some better argument is needed, and I am

[6] *Ibid.*, p. lii.
[7] For a discussion of these views, see my *Analytical Philosophy of Knowledge* (Cambridge, England, 1968), ch. 4.

## Nothingness: or, Consciousness and Ontology | 53

not certain I can provide one. Perhaps one might reason this way: nothing can be part of the contents of my consciousness without my being conscious of it: nothing can be *in* consciousness *of* which I am not conscious. Then, if consciousness is part of its own contents, I would be conscious of it. But does consciousness really contain itself as a proper part? Is the container, as it were, part of its own contents? It does not seem, on Sartrian ground, that it can be. For then consciousness would be amongst its own objects and by definition *could* exist apart from one's being conscious of it: this is just the contrary of what Sartre needs to prove. In any case, Sartre wants to say that consciousness of consciousness is *not* "objective," that consciousness is never *of* itself as it is of apples or some other sort of object: consciousness of consciousness is not *objective* consciousness at all. Sartre marks the distinction by putting "of" in parentheses: it is *concience (de) soi*, in contrast to *conscience de—*. The latter he speaks of as objective or reflective consciousness, and the former as *prereflective* consciousness, which is always only of itself.

That there must be some difference between knowing that I am conscious and knowing something exists because I am conscious of it, is something for which Sartre has perhaps a better argument. Suppose all consciousness were objective. Then I know an apple is there because I am conscious of it. And I know that I am conscious of an apple being there by being conscious of this bit of consciousness. But then how do I know that I am conscious of this consciousness of consciousness? Presumably by being conscious of the fact—and plainly this generates an infinite regression, which would mean that I am finally incapable of knowing that I am conscious at all. Yet the argument only entails that if I am conscious of being conscious, I must be so in some immediate and direct way. It does not entail that if I am conscious of anything, I must be directly and immediately conscious of being so, which is the conclusion he would have wanted. The former argument, then, does not yield the conclusion Sartre requires, that: "there must be an immediate, noncognitive relation of the self to itself."[8] Whatever the case, the latter, in contrast to the reflective consciousness I have of objects, is prereflective or nonpositional. To be (positionally) conscious of $x$ is to be (nonpositionally) conscious that one is so. Consider Sartre's illustrative use of the concept of counting at this point. To count my cigarettes implies that I do not know how many there are and mean to find out. But I do not find out in the same sense that I am counting: I am immediately aware of this; and this prereflective awareness that counting is what I am doing is presupposed by the actual act of adding which I perform. It is what unites the repetitions as part of a single project.

The upshot is that the structure of consciousness itself is very different from the structure of the objects of consciousness. Of course, I *can* be aware of myself in the same way in which I am aware of objects, can be an object for myself, and Sartre admits, indeed requires as much in his early important study, the *Transcendence of the Ego*. But this cannot, in terms of his philosophy be the sole, nor can it be the philosophically main way in which I am conscious of myself, and in fact it is possible that I should be conscious of myself without ever becoming an object of my consciousness or realizing that I can. How it should happen that I acquire

[8] *Being and Nothingness*, p. liii.

this status as an object must be approached through an analysis of the *être-pour-autrui*, but were it somehow true that the only consciousness I had of myself was as an object, or through objective consciousness, a serious problem would arise as to how I should know that what I was aware of was *myself*, more intimately related to me than the other objects which swim before awareness; this would be like a certain form of schizophrenia. It is, then, the prereflective awareness that I am the thing of which I am aware, that I am the awareness— so that subject and object, as far as these terms apply here at all, are one—which is the main delivered content of this mode of consciousness.

Another (more typically Sartrian) point should be made here, since it connects with Sartre's notions of spontaneity. To be aware of $x$ positionally is to believe that $x$ is independent of my consciousness of it, and that it existed or at least could have existed anterior to the moment of this awareness. But this makes no sense whatever for the prereflective awareness of awareness itself: the latter cannot exist independently of the former, nor predate it: "consciousness is not *possible* before being," Sartre writes, and so "its existence implies its essence."[9] It is there, as it were, before we are aware of its being anything other than the awareness itself. We can put this in a different light. I am aware of being pleased. But being pleased is not something I stumble upon, which might have been there whether I had been aware of it or not, after the manner of a table. So again it is not as though I *become* aware of being pleased. Being pleased coexists with its own awareness: pleasure and awareness of pleasure are

[9] *Ibid.*, p. lv.

stitchlessly united in a single compound, like the members of the trinity.[10] This is why I think, Sartre, is so opposed to what he terms the Unconscious, at least as it is employed in psychoanalytical theory. For unconscious beliefs or feelings *are* beliefs and feelings I may or can "stumble onto," things I might never have known about myself. I am, in a way aware of them in my own case as I am in the case of an other, positionally and reflectively.

Even so, Sartre has room in his thought for such a possibility, and since it gives endless philosophical trouble to him, we might pause to consider its ramifications. In the *Transcendence of the Ego*, he developed an impressive argument against his master Husserl, which is in a way reminiscent of Hume's argument regarding the self. Husserl believed, and came increasingly to believe, in the existence of an ego which, as it were, stands outside its experiences it instead "owns." Sartre found this positing of an absolute ego quite unacceptable. The self certainly exists, he claimed, but it is an object within the phenomenal field, as much as any. "The ego is not the owner of consciousness, it is the object of consciousness." And "our states and actions are also objects."[11] He quotes approvingly from Rimbaud: "I *is* an Other." Within the system in which there is an ego, with allegedly immediate access to its states, the states of Others are open to no such cognitive privilege and can be construed either as unknowable or at best as available only through some treacherous inferential process, based on a kind of analogy. But in this new

---

[10] "Pleasure can not be distinguished—even logically—from consciousness of pleasure." *Ibid.*, p. liv.

[11] *The Transcendence of the Ego*, trans. Forrest Williams and Robert Kirkpatrick, p. 97.

## Nothingness: or, Consciousness and Ontology | 57

view, Sartre supposes, if I and Pierre should speak of my love for Anny, we speak of the same thing and know the same thing, as much an object for me as for him, an object no more certain for me than for him. To be sure, it is "my" emotion. But if we put the emotion into consciousness, it draws the *me* into consciousness as well: if it is an object for consciousness, the "me" is so as well. "The method of internal introspection and the method of external observation have the same rights, and naturally can assist one another."[12] The self and its feelings are transcendent, and essentially public. But why should it not then be possible for states of a person which, as is allegedly so with unconscious feelings and beliefs, not to be prereflectively available to him, but available only through the sorts of "external observation" which the processes of psychoanalysis enhance, or is supposed to? My unconscious, if it exists, is no less an "other" than someone else's feelings and beliefs. What can be the objection? It can be objected against only if the self and its states are *withdrawn* from the domain of objects and reintroduced, contrary to the teaching of the book, as modes of consciousness. But the point of the teaching is to purge consciousness of all such states, so that there is no "inner life" and everything heretofore relegated to it exists "out there," in a region of the phenomenal field, so that consciousness itself is a kind of pure transparency, a "nothing" which is merely an openness to a world to which it adds no tincture of its own.

This is exactly the view of a totally evacuated consciousness which Sartre develops in *Being and Nothingness*. In a way the example of pleasure which he gives there was wrongly stated: pleasure, too, is an object

[12] *Ibid.*

rather than a state of consciousness, and as an object may be had without being aware of it (even if, when indeed I am aware of pleasure, I am aware that I am). No structural difference exists between my awareness of being pleased and my awareness that I am aware of a table, except such objective differences as may divide tables from pleasures. Moreover, it remains a possibility that I should be aware of something and hence aware that I am without being *reflectively*, "positionally," conscious of my state. A major difficulty, as we shall see, in Sartre's philosophy of consciousness, is that there is a difference between prereflective self-awareness and reflective self-awareness, and the argument that we must be aware of awareness when we are aware at all entails nothing about reflective consciousness. And what more than this distinction do we require for the possibility of an unconscious, namely that there should be things of which I am aware, and hence prereflectively aware, but of which I have no *reflective* consciousness whatever?

Let us, without protracting these difficulties, sum up the matter this way. Consciousness always is of objects which the possessor of consciousness is constrained to regard as real things. These then are believed to be independent of consciousness and to exist in themselves. But there is no consciousness which is independent of any object at all, for consciousness logically presupposes something independent of itself in order that it should exist, and so does *not*, in the required sense, exist *en-soi*. But it does exist for itself, in the sense that I am always aware of being aware when I am aware, and I always am aware insofar as I am a conscious being. This, then, is the structural geography of consciousness, from which the ontological distinctions follow. They are complicated by the fact that as a self, I may also be

## Nothingness: or, Consciousness and Ontology | 59

an object for myself; that I may not be aware of my objective status; and that when I am an object for myself, the consciousness appealed to is not prereflective but reflective. What remains now is to explicate the further connections between those distinct regions of being which have been internally marked off through this analysis.

Since we are operating from within consciousness, it is not easy to suppose that a single sense of "existence" is common to the two orders of being. For things *en-soi*, the meaning of "existence" is that they have aspects not immediately given to experience. To exist in this sense as a *pour-soi* is to think that there are *now* aspects of consciousness not immediately given, and as these would be tantamount to states of consciousness of which we are not conscious, there *would* be a kind of unconscious. Sartre has neither room nor taste for such a notion. Again, the *en-soi* exists independently of one's consciousness of it, but *consciousness* cannot exist this way. There is a third difference, of which Sartre makes a good deal, namely that an *en-soi* "is what it is." If the *pour-soi* is so totally different from the *en-soi*, as Sartre supposes, it must *not* be what it is, and Sartre says as much. Such a formulation seems insane on the face of it—as though humans, unlike things, were not subject to the Law of Identity. It is nevertheless a characterization of the *pour-soi* upon which Sartre insists strongly, and we can do no better than to follow out its implications if we are to appreciate what Sartre wants to say about us. This will bring us close to the concept of nothingness. It is already plain that consciousness admits a kind of negative characterization. It has no qualities or states of its own, being always of something to which it is logically external. Hence it has no location in the world of things, say as some specially diaphanous entity: it is not part of the objective order. What can it be, and what can be its relation to the world it is at once attached to and outside?

The very posing of the question, rather than the specific question posed, reveals, Sartre believes, a great deal about the being that does the posing, and his thought here is extremely suggestive. Heidegger put forward a view that man is the being for whom his being is in question: the query What am I? (What are we?) gets a kind of answer through the mere fact that it is asked: we are the kind of being for which it is possible to wonder what one is, and this may be a deeper structural fact about ourselves than any answer to the question itself might give; certainly no answer can be given that does not take into account everything conceptually required by the existence of a being the nature of whose existence is a conceptual problem for himself. Dogs (one hopes) face no such problem of identity, however conscious they may be of the world. Sartre puts the matter somewhat differently and rather more linguistically. "The moment when I ask 'Is there any conduct which can reveal to me the relation of myself with the world?' I admit *in principle* the possibility of a negative reply." To ask the question, indeed to ask any question, is to be in a state of indeterminance. From this, Sartre dramatically concludes, "The permanent possibility of non-being, outside us and within us, conditions our question about being."[13] He insists that this is not merely a subjective state of affairs, a matter of not knowing what is the case. For there is a possibility of knowing what is not the case, knowing what we might call a negative fact; this is as objective a piece

[13] *Being and Nothingness*, p. 5.

## Nothingness: or, Consciousness and Ontology | 61

of knowledge as any, and with it non-being, objective negativity, appears as "a new component of the real."

Actually, were Sartre more liberated from Heideggerian postures, the point could have been made with grammatical forms other than interrogations. Assertions are either true or false, so to make an assertion is to face the possibility of being wrong, and this, when one comes to know it, means that one knows now what was not the case: namely what one believed it was when one made the assertion. Or an imperative generates the possibilities alike of being obeyed or disobeyed. These negative matters, let us stress, are relative to language or to thought, since it is only in relation to a question or assertion or command that they arise. It is not clear that the world in itself contains negations that would be there whether we were conscious of them or not, like antimatter or negative electricity. So it is only in a qualified sense, and relative to us as questioners or describers, that non-being in this sense emerges at all. But Sartre accepts this and affirms it: "It would be in vain," he writes, "to deny that negation appears on the original basis of a relation of man to the world."[14] And again, "Non-being always appears within the limits of a human expectation." And since non-being presupposes a relation, it is not a property of either of the things related: not an absolute trait of the world; nor is it a kind of hole in consciousness; nor is it due to some special grammatical feature of language, as in logical negation or in negative propositions (the latter are either true or false, and so generate the possibility of a negativity other than that expressed in the proposition itself).

Sartre makes the point with the example of destruc-

[14] *Ibid.*, p. 7.

tion, characteristically saying, in a way that has to be literally false, "man is the only being by whom a destruction can be accomplished."[15] This is true not in the sense that the rest of nature is benign and preservative and only man the nihilating energy within it— there are, after all, storms and floods and epidemics and fires—but rather in the sense that we can speak of destruction meaningfully only in relation to human hopes and beliefs: otherwise there are just rearrangements of matter. A city before and after an earthquake simply reveals different states as far as the laws of physics are concerned. So "destruction" is a relational concept, where one of the terms of the relationship is a human being or set of human beings who stand to gain or lose by the objective change—after all, we are largely indifferent to the coming and going of sunspots, since there is no human investment in these. And so again with the concept of "fragility,"—"fragility enter(s) into . . . being as the appearance of a permanent possibility of non-being."[16] The concept of nothingness in the relevant sense is built into our very vocabulary, and the claim that only through man is there destruction is a conceptual rather than a causal claim, on the basis of which we then can accept with equanimity the otherwise startling proposition, "*it is man* who destroys his cities through the agency of earthquakes or directly, who destroys his ships through . . . cyclones. . . ."[17] Sartre illustrates this, finally, in one of his most famous passages, where he describes going to a café to meet Pierre, who proves not to be there. The café itself is a "fullness of being," even, we might add, if it has holes

---

[15] *Ibid.*, p. 8.
[16] *Ibid.*
[17] *Ibid.*, p. 9.

## Nothingness: or, Consciousness and Ontology | 63

in the linoleum and a leaking ceiling. It is only with respect to one's anticipations of Pierre's being there that he is not. One can, abstractly, make all sorts of negative descriptions of the café: Victor Hugo is not there, nor Charles Parsons, nor the Emperor of Ice Cream. These are mere thoughts, negative descriptions rather than negations made through the act of judging. It is the defeat of an expectation rather than the satisfaction of a negative belief which is in issue: we are dealing, so to speak, not with the absence of a presence but the presence of an absence, and I am conscious of the absence because I genuinely expected a presence. So Pierre's not being there, as Sartre will predictably say, is *my* responsibility, not Pierre's. If he was delayed though I had not expected him, his not being there would not be an object of awareness for me, nor a relevant negativity with regard to my consciousness at all. It is because of the constant possibility of dashed hopes and thwarted expectations, then, that "nothingness haunts being." But, of course, though Sartre never pauses to think about the matter, Pierre's *being* there would also be relative to an expectation of consciousness. There are all sorts of people in the café whose presence is as irrelevant as the absence of the enormous number of people to whom I am indifferent: there is a sense of being which is logically on the same footing with the sense of nothingness Sartre makes so central. Were he a more affirmative spirit, he might have made the same point, less excitingly, to be sure, by insisting that man is the only *constructive* being in the world, making grain through the agency of germination.

Heidegger, in a passage of sustained mystical urgency, wrote about the experience of nothingness in *What Is Metaphysics?* It comes at moments of cosmic boredom, moments when all distinctions flatten out; a boredom that we know in advance cannot be removed, because it is metaphysical rather than the affective ennui of a dull afternoon we can at least hope will be broken, because it comes in the dark night of the soul. *Then* we encounter nothingness as the boundary of being, rather than as a demarcation within being, and it evidently requires a perception of totality and hence of boundaries before it can come to consciousness. Sartre concedes that "non-being exists only on the surface of things," meaning, I expect, that nothingness is not a special kind of something, not a *kind* of thing. But, and this is consistent with his form of thinking, he does not suppose that we arrive at a consciousness of nothingness only at extreme moments of the sort Heidegger pointed to. We may never *have* that kind of experience—in which, in a phrase which became a stock example of nonsense in the merry heyday of logical positivism, "Nothing noths." "How can this extra-mundane nothingness furnish a foundation for those little pools of non-being which we encounter each instant in the depth of being?"[18] I find that Pierre is not in the café, or that I have no money, or that the letter has not come. And it is these experiences which reveal nothingness to me, rather than that global experience in which the boundaries of reality as a whole are shatteringly unveiled to an essentially religious apprehension. Sartre speaks of these domestic nothingnesses as *"négatités,"* dispersed throughout the world insofar as one lives in it. So Heidegger's account is too grand, too beyond routine experience in which nothingness arises in a daily, general way. A *child* knows it when he knows the meaning of disappointment: he acquires the concept when he acquires speech.

[18] *Ibid.*, p. 19.

## Nothingness: or, Consciousness and Ontology | 65

It is important, because of the misconceptions to which this notion has given life, that we stress that nothingness is not an entity. "Nothingness 'is made to be,'"[19] as Sartre puts it; it is a kind of shadow that we cast rather than an antecedent vacuity that we discover. And this tells us, he believes, a great deal about the sort of beings we are, which is presumably why he makes so much of it in his exposition and why he might have been unable to make the same characterization with the quite collateral use of "being" alluded to above: for "being" may have two senses, one of an antecedent reality, independent of human thought or action, and the other that of "made-to-be." But nothingness has only *one* sense. So let us follow the exposition out.

"Nothing comes from nothing" is a sad utterance we associate with Lear. But *ex nihilo nihil fit* is an ancient metaphysical thesis, a form of the Principle of Sufficient Reason, according to which a reason exists for whatever takes place; nothing occurs without an adequate explanation. Sartre puns on this, saying in effect that nothingness cannot come from something, so that nothingness cannot be an effect of being or have its explanation in the *en-soi*. Being only produces more being. So nothingness can only (literally) be produced by nothing. And since it is through *us* that nothingness appears in the world, *we* must be a nothingness of sorts. *"The being by which Nothingness comes to the world must be its own Nothingness,"*[20] to repeat a phrase which now has its context. And this will prove to be the deep basis for Sartre's notion of freedom. For the ideas of freedom and nothingness are exceedingly closely re-

---

[19] *Ibid.*, p. 22. This is Dr. Barnes's way of translating Sartre's ungrammatical *est été*.
[20] *Ibid.*, p. 23.

lated in Sartre's system, which is why he is justified in beginning his major work with a treatment of the origin of negation—not as an exercise in the philosophy of logic, since as we saw negation has nothing to do either with the content of propositions or with operations on propositions such as denial; nor as a kind of psychological analysis, since negation is not a kind of mental state like doubt or a feeling of emptiness; nor, finally, is it a kind of objective vacuity, like nirvana. Since it is none of these things and yet seems to be an ingredient in even the most ordinary experiences, some analysis of it is called for; yet it is not simply a thing which a philosopher has a certain responsibility to get clear along with other ingredients of experience—though it may in fact be said that philosophers before Sartre have neglected or misappreciated it. Rather, it is bound up with the nature and structure of consciousness, and the claim is made that we cannot fully understand what we are until it has been worked out. And now we are going to try to give some further definition to the concepts of consciousness and nothingness alike, by examining the concept of freedom.

In Sartre's view, consciousness is characterized by a certain sort of spontaneity, which we are in part to understand through the formula that its existence precedes its essence. In *The Transcendence of the Ego*, he claims that "it determines its existence at each moment, without our being able to conceive anything before it. Thus each moment of our conscious life reveals to us a creation *ex nihilo*."[21] This spontaneity has nothing to do with the will, not merely (he argues) because we must

[21] *The Transcendence of the Ego*, pp. 98–99.

first be conscious before we can will anything, but because the will itself is an object of consciousness and not part of its structure. So our spontaneity is not something over which we have any control. It is not something which can be or not be, the way I can raise my arm or leave it where it is.

Consider the first moment at which consciousness exists. It obviously cannot be caused by some prior state of itself, for by hypothesis this *is* its first state. But neither can it be caused by a thing, since it is not a thing, and things can only be invoked in the explanation of things. Consciousness is causally independent of everything. To be sure, it is dependent upon the world in another way, as we have already discussed, insofar as it requires an object. But the object only determines the content of consciousness, not its existence. Consciousness is a spontaneity as far as anything within or outside itself is concerned, and to apply causal notions to it is exactly to treat it as though it were a thing.

This sounds extraordinary and false. Surely, it will be argued, we *can* explain the conditions under which consciousness arises and under which it disappears: a blow to the head or a deprivation of oxygen will snuff it out. But it must be recalled that we are exploring the logical structures of consciousness, and from within. We are exploring what, given that we are conscious, we are required to believe about it and its objects. Science, too, is something which is an object of consciousness, and so exists within the field of consciousness and presupposes a structure which it cannot then call in question. But it is then through an internal analysis of consciousness that we have arrived at this notion of its spontaneity. Sartre is again being conceptual rather than causal, so let us remain within the framework of phenomenology, instead of going outside it, it being with reference to the external position that the objection was raised.

Sartre's argument here is extremely tortured, and I would be pleased to omit it in a work of this sort were it not bound up with so absolutely indispensable a notion. But perhaps we can work it out this way (which will incidentally explain why his thesis about prereflexive consciousness of consciousness is so important to him). Consciousness (*c*) is always distinct from its objects, is never identical with whatever it is of—or at least this is so with reflective consciousness. This is a fact about consciousness, but in one sense there are no *external* facts about consciousness. That is to say, whatever is true of consciousness is something we are automatically conscious of as true. If F is a property of consciousness, then we are conscious of F, usually prereflectively. There is thus a kind of formula we might use: $F(c)$ entails $c(F)$, and conversely: whatever is the case with consciousness is something we are conscious is the case. So if consciousness is *not-x*, where *x* is the object of consciousness, its *non-x-ness* is necessarily something of which we are conscious. Thus, to be conscious of a tree is to be conscious of the fact that the consciousness in question is not the tree; rather, it is merely *of* the tree. This is so whatever may be the object of consciousness, even if the object should be one's objective self. But we *are* what we are conscious of being. So what we are is, for any object of consciousness *x*, *not-x*. And nihilation in this way is the very being of consciousness. We are a constant and unending nihilation of anything which may be an object of consciousness.

It is exactly in this sense, then, that consciousness is a kind of nothingness: not an absolute lack, an un-

## Nothingness: or, Consciousness and Ontology | 69

qualified nihility, but a transitive one; a not-this, a not-that, for any given this or that. Put in these terms, Sartre's otherwise perverse formula even makes direct sense: "we are what we are not." We are not our objects. To be sure, there are many things we are not, but reference to them does not enter into the direct description of consciousness unless they become objects for it. So Smith may not be a tree, but this does not form a description of Smith's consciousness until the tree is an object of his consciousness, at which point what he is, as a consciousness, is not-that-tree. The phrase "I am what I am not" must be understood in the specific sense of *not-being-x*. And this is the sense in which the *pour-soi* contrasts with the *en-soi* when the latter are characterized as being what they are.

Of course, the entire argument is a kind of logical spoof. We are, are identical with, these various nihilations, if Sartre's analysis is at all correct, in just the way a stone is identical with itself. "Nihilation $n$ is identical with nihilation $n$" is as good an instance of the Principle of Identity, as "Stone $s$ is identical with stone $s$" is. So the first "is" in "the *pour-soi* is what it is not" is just the "is" of identity. Still, the fact remains (if it is a fact) that what we are identical with is a set of nihilations, of not-being-somethings. It is not in Sartre's nature to pass up the sort of logical obfuscations which make up the textures of a play by Tom Stoppard.

The $F(c)=c(F)$ scheme is a very powerful one for Sartre, and it yields some striking results. For instance, if, as consciousness, we are indeed free, then we must be conscious of being so. Men have disputed whether there is a consciousness of freedom, and what it might mean for the free-will controversy if there were or were not such a consciousness. Perhaps they were seeking for this sense of feeling as an *object* rather than as a trait of consciousness; if it is an object, then some men might have it and others not, whereas if it is a trait of consciousness, we must be conscious of the trait. And the latter is indeed Sartre's view, so much so that he could write, in the *Transcendence of the Ego*, that our spontaneity is "beyond freedom."[22] I take him to mean that it has nothing to do with anything of which we are conscious of in the world of objects. But then, if spontaneity is a trait of consciousness, and by the formula is accordingly something of which we are conscious, the issue ought to be capable of immediate resolution through an immediate prereflective consciousness of the trait. Unfortunately, it does not follow from the fact that we are prereflectively conscious of freedom that we are *reflectively* so, and so at the level at which philosophical controversies are enacted, prereflective consciousness is of little aid. In some way it must be demonstrated at the reflective level that we *have* this prereflective consciousness, for not everyone is aware that we do. And we may see this in considering Sartre's key notion of anguish.

Anguish, as Sartre employs the concept, is the *reflective* consciousness of freedom. If it is a feeling at all, it has nothing to do with the sort of agony or apprehension we may have when we are afraid or desperate or anxious—if only because these, as is consistent with Sartre's philosophy of mind, are objects of consciousness rather than ways of being conscious. Anguish is a way of being conscious. Moreover, Sartre argues, anguish and fear are mutually exclusive, anguish having solely to do with oneself, with the fact that what one does is up to oneself, whereas fear concerns what might happen to oneself, and from without. But, as always, matters

[22] *Ibid.*

# Nothingness: or, Consciousness and Ontology | 71

are more complex than Sartre's examples—of a soldier reporting to war, or a man treading the dangerous edge of a precipice—imply, anguish having to do with the structures of consciousness. The somewhat charged and emotional overtones of the term will dissipate when we see precisely what the intended concept amounts to. Essentially, it concerns the relationship between what I am at a given instant, and what I have been and will be. Hence it exactly concerns the concept of spontaneity, the connection the *pour-soi* has to its past and future. This relationship is going predictably to be nihilative— "as being both this past and future and as not being them."[23] Let us first consider this from the direction of present to future. Mountain-climbing, I find myself at the edge of an abyss, suddenly afraid of falling to my death. But because I am afraid, because I internalize the situation as revealed by fear, I begin moving more carefully, watching my steps. As I do so, the world becomes transformed into a set of possibilities *I* control through choice and action. These possibilities are not resident in the *en-soi*; rather they constitute what Sartre speaks of as my *situation*, of which I am the source. Sartre means by situation an active structuring of the world from the perspective of an engaged consciousness, and he has aptly used the term as the title of his various reprinted essays. But his philosophical point will be that since I am responsible for the possibilities being there, they cannot determine what I do in any causal way: it is always up to me which possibility is to be actualized. Nevertheless, the I who will do the actualizing is a future state of me—not me now, for whom it is just a possibility and not a fact. And I am not (temporally) that future me. To be sure, it is not as though an alto-

[23] *Being and Nothingness*, p. 29.

gether different person will do the actualizing, so there is an internal link of some sort. Sartre's way of putting it is this: "I am the self I will be in the mode of not being it." But, "the decisive conduct will emanate from a self which I am not yet."[24] Thus the self which I am (continuously) will depend upon the self which I am (temporally) not. And nothing I now do can possibly foreclose what I will do a moment hence. So, in a curious metaphysical way, and due to the fact that I cannot occupy two times at once, because instantaneity is my mode of temporal being, I *am* helpless before the future.

This structure, let us note, is perfectly general, and applies in far less dramatic cases than walking along a cliff. Thus what or whether I write a moment hence, what or whether I eat an hour from now, exemplify the same structure though they hardly involve the same feelings. Even so, anguish describes my apprehension of this rather banal fact about time and choice. We must not, here more than elsewhere, allow the dramatic extremity of the examples to bias the philosophical purport of the concepts they happen to illustrate: as a literary artist, Sartre has the taste of a teller of adventurous tales, and relishes the sort of suspense we find in comic strips.

His example of the past-present direction is, on the other hand, profound. He describes a gambler who has resolved to gamble no more, and who now finds himself at the gaming table.[25] He finds that yesterday's decision constrains him not at all, unless he *now* decides to honor it—and this is simply a fresh decision. It is almost as though someone else had made the earlier one. I

[24] *Ibid.*, p. 32.
[25] *Ibid.*, pp. 32–33.

## Nothingness: or, Consciousness and Ontology | 73

face the present virtually as a new being, having to choose all over. Apt as it is, the example merely dramatizes the fact that decisions must always be made, but when the decision is enacted it will be through a self as distant from me now as I now am from my past self.

The consciousness of freedom is anguish: "anguish in its essential structure as consciousness of freedom."[26] The examples, however, and the fact that we may need them only underscore the fact, only bring this structural fact about spontaneity to (reflective) consciousness. So this consciousness cannot be anything of the sort automatically guaranteed by the $F(c)=c(F)$ schematism. Since the latter is inalienable, I must always be conscious of freedom if consciousness is free, hence always be in anguish if this is what anguish comes to, even if it is a matter of taking a second *croissant* or lying down to snooze. But Sartre explicitly says, "the most common situations of our life . . . do not manifest themselves to us through anguish because their very structure excludes anguished apprehension."[27] This may be so. But then "apprehension" cannot mean anything like the prereflective consciousness which the $F(c)=c(F)$ formula implies. And since the only alternative to that mode of consciousness is objective or reflective consciousness, it ought to have reference to some external structure, from which, according to the analysis, I must stand at a certain distance, or must nihilate. I do not in fact see any way of fitting *this* sort of consciousness in Sartre's scheme at all. In his architectural rendering of consciousness he has curiously neglected what he appears mainly to talk about in his phenomenology, namely, the sort of reflective consciousness which the *pour-soi* attains

[26] *Ibid.*, p. 33.
[27] *Ibid.*, p. 35.

to of itself, a kind of consciousness that, it seems to me, prereflective consciousness has nothing to do with. For the way in which I represent myself through this sort of reflective consciousness—the way I am *for* myself here, is *not* entailed by prereflective awareness. But that Sartre requires such a structure should be clear from the phenomenon of "bad faith," which is an implicit denial of freedom and a way of fleeing anguish. He evidently felt this as a difficulty, however, since he immediately goes on to consider bad faith in his exposition of consciousness, and I want now to discuss this, for it is one of his most interesting ideas.

Since the idea of anguish plays so prominent a role in existentialist writing, as much in Kierkegaard and Heidegger as in Sartre, a word more on it may be in order. To begin with, it is rather an elitist and philosophical feeling and has little if anything to do with those states in which as ordinary men we are dismayed by the danger and harshness of life, and which may be called anguish: with the feelings one has when a letter does not come, or a child is sick, or one's job or country is threatened. We hardly need philosophers to tell us that life is anguishing in that sense. And, in any case, this sort of anguish is transient and sporadic, whereas the sort of anguish to which the existentialists allude has reference to the whole of human existence and not just to dark episodes which may or may not come up in it. Its content, what it is about, is human freedom, at least in Kierkegaard and Sartre, and it is about nothingness in Heidegger; we may recall that the encounter with nothingness was a rare, even privileged experience in *What Is Metaphysics?* Not everyone sustains what we may now term metaphysical anguish, even if every-

## Nothingness: or, Consciousness and Ontology | 75

one is free and prereflectively aware of being so. "It is," Sartre writes, "completely exceptional."[28] It is, in a way, available only to those who come to a reflective consciousness of their freedom, however this is done, and who recognize that we ourselves are "the original source of [our] possibility"[29] or, more dramatically, that we make our own *world*. I have labored to argue that if it were merely a matter of prereflective consciousness, everyone would be anguished, and this is what is explicitly denied. So how are we to appreciate the kind of consciousness which is required? Perhaps the matter could be simply taken care of if we considered that anguish was in the end just a philosophical belief about the structure of our being, a true belief if Sartre's analysis is correct, though not one whose truth is spontaneously brought home to us through the structures he has analyzed. This would make bad faith a matter of a false philosophical belief, and there is no mystery in how someone might arrive at it. For since the structures of consciousness do not compel the reflective awareness of themselves the way they compel prereflective awareness, it is wholly consistent that man might have a wrong reflective awareness of a condition which *prereflectively* he was aware was quite otherwise. Against this way of seeing things, let us examine what the content of bad faith is.

Anguish is the recognition that things have the meanings we give them, that the system of meanings through which we define our situation from moment to moment are assigned to the world through us, and that we cannot then derive them from the way the world is (i.e.,

---

[28] *Ibid.*
[29] *Ibid.*, p. 41.

*en-soi*). So each of us is responsible for the world he lives in. Let us recall that the spirit of seriousness for which Roquentin condemned the burghers of Bouville is precisely the reverse of this view, namely, that meanings are resident in things, woven into the objective fabric of the universe: "the meaning which my freedom has given to the world, I apprehend as coming from the world." Anguish is the contrary intuition and, presumably, the correct one: "I apprehend myself . . . as totally free and as not being able to derive the meaning of the world except as coming from myself."[30] The concept of anguish will have a special, crucial role to play in connection with the concept of values, but I shall put that topic in parentheses until the end of this book. All I want here to stress is that bad faith is a case of the spirit of seriousness, with one special difference. Men may believe in the philosophy of seriousness without ever having known or thought otherwise. And nothing, I have argued, in the structure of the *pour-soi* need ever require them to believe otherwise. Never having risen to the level of anguish, they have no anguish to escape or to try to escape. Whereas bad faith is just that: an attempt to repudiate in our lives what we know is false in our philosophy, to live as though the serious view is true when we know it to be false. Hence it is a kind of self-deception. Sartre regards psychological determinism, for example, when an avowed theory, as an attempt to flee anguish because it regards the modes of consciousness as though they were objects, susceptible to causal determinism. "Thus we flee from anguish by attempting to apprehend ourselves from without as an Other or as *a thing*."[31] Bad faith, then, is the

[30] *Ibid.*, pp. 39–40.
[31] *Ibid.*, p. 43.

generic label for all such attitudes. And since we must somehow know the position from which we are trying to flee, Sartre can plausibly write that "the flight from anguish is only a mode of becoming conscious of anguish," so "It is certain that we cannot overcome anguish"[32]—though this seems to imply a yet higher level of consciousness than any we so far have had to mark. Still, to the degree that anguish is "exceptional," so must bad faith be. And it is not plain that those maligned bourgeois in fact exemplify it: they may never have known better. We can only repudiate what we are aware is there to be repudiated. So bad faith does not have the polemical force or quite the polemic force Sartre believes it to have.

Sartre's examples of bad faith are, as usual, striking and persuasive. A waiter tries to be a waiter as though waiterhood were his very essence, as though he were a waiter the way a turnip is a turnip, having no choice in the matter. It is, then, an attempt, presumably doomed, to flatten himself into a kind of thing, and to disguise the fact that being a waiter, and going on being one, is a choice he makes, a choice which must be from moment to moment reaffirmed through his actions and through the situations his choices generate. This may, as I say, be a case of self-deception. But it is so only if the waiter has already internalized the substance of the philosophy of Sartre. True, he may still never succeed in being a waiter in the required way, simply because it is not given to human beings to be objects in the required way. But though the enterprise is somehow wrong, it is not a gesture of bad faith because the waiter may never have attained in the first place to a conscious awareness that this is the nature of men. He

[32] *Ibid.*

is deceived but not *self*-deceived. It is, I think, a logical presupposition of the notion of self-deception that a man deceives himself only if he knows the truth. One can be self-deceived under the form of bad faith only if one knows already that one is free. But one may not know this, not even if it is the truth and not even if one in fact is prereflectively aware that one is. There is no philosophical difficulty in analyzing those cases in which there is a conflict between prereflective and reflective consciousness, because in the end they involve no self-deception at all. And this fault infects most of the examples by means of which Sartre undertakes to illustrate bad faith. In all of them the people are deceived about themselves without necessarily being self-deceived. Indeed, there may not be any genuine instances of bad faith. True, some philosophers believe that the distinction between human beings and mere things comes to very little. They believe that human beings are subject to just the same sorts of determinism which allegedly reign in the (merely) physical order. They may be wrong. But their being so is not necessarily Bad Faith, just wrong philosophy. To be sure, they are aware that some philosophies hold a view contrary to their own, like Sartre's, for example. But it would be false to say they *know* these antithetical philosophies to be true and are seeking through their own to escape this recognition. They will deny this. They may say that the antithetical philosophies are an attempt to flee our essential objecthood in a false conception of freedom, that *Sartre* is the practioner rather than they of bad faith. No doubt there *are* cases of self-deception. But there is no need here to undertake the difficult task of rendering them philosophically perspicuous, since it is not clear that the false philosophy of his opponents, if it is that, falls

## Nothingness: or, Consciousness and Ontology | 79

under bad faith, and Sartre has no argument to show that it does. All we need do is recognize that bad faith presupposes what Sartre believes to be false philosophy, namely, that men are like things—but this philosophy, false as it may be, does not entail bad faith.

The mechanisms of anguish and bad faith together are really, then, external to the main structures of consciousness which Sartre goes to such pains to identify in the first crucial pages of *Being and Nothingness*. They are deep and interesting notions, but they are not in any way necessitated by those structures, nor are those structures somehow self-validating. Anguish and bad faith, one might say, belong less to the structures of consciousness than to those of the intellect, and they refer us to the sorts of general descriptions we may give of human life, bad faith being perhaps a false description of the sort we discussed in connection with *Nausea*: by wrongly believing oneself to be on a footing with things, one misses the authentic perception of one's life which it is the mission of philosophical understanding to furnish. But we may utilize the concept of bad faith to complete by indirection what Sartre wanted to say is the nature of the *pour-soi*. We have seen already in what sense it may be said to be what it is not. But now we can also say, inasmuch as the distance between a man and the roles he may play cannot be overcome, that a man never *is* a waiter or a husband or a father or a philosopher or whatever, that a man *is not* what he *is*. Taking the first "is" as that of identity, and the second "is" as that of predication, it is false in the first use that Jean is a waiter, even if true in the second sense, even if, as a matter of calling, a waiter is what he is. The two formulations together then express what

Sartre condenses in the rather infuriating formula: "Men are what they are not and are not what they are."

There is one further point to make. Possibly the recognition of the truth of this formula and of all that it implies will be *felt* with anguish. It may, for instance, so be felt by those who once believed otherwise and now realize they cannot shirk the responsibility for their lives and indeed their world. Coming now to believe the old view to be false, they may in fact feel a sense of loss or alienation. Or they may not. They may instead have a feeling of liberation and exultation. But the structure which Sartre has identified is invariant to its affective accompaniments and cannot be translated into them, and so the meaning of "anguish" is really far more neutral than its ordinary use would imply. This is meant less as an objection than a helpful observation.

On the other hand, and here the suitability of the term may after all reside, Sartre supposes that this view of utter freedom is a difficult one to live with, and that men always do have a propensity to try to cast the burden off, to live as though they were settled objects, to look for excuses for their conduct in a world they have in fact themselves made and so are responsible for. If we are defined by a freedom and also by the propensity to cast it off, then indeed the meaning of our lives is a perpetual anguish, for we cannot at once be this freedom and not be it, cannot at once be conscious and be a thing. The attempt to impose upon ourselves the order of description which pertains to things, as well as the contrary, are radical examples of the discrepancies which exist between the way men represent the world and the way it is. To live with the truth, as Sartre believes he has stated it in *Being and Nothingness*, is, I suppose, to affirm anguish, and this we might call Good Faith. And it may indeed be the truth, though I am afraid I see no way, on the basis of that book, to settle the matter one way rather than another.

# Engagement: or, Knowledge, Action, and the World

# iii

The great framework of distinctions which makes up Martin Heidegger's monumental work *Being and Time* seeps palimpsestically through the pages of *Being and Nothingness*. It is no secret that *Being and Time* deeply influenced Sartre, both in the conception of the singularly Teutonic book he wrote, and in the content of that work, so that critics have assigned Sartre a far lower degree of originality than he merits as a philosopher. In any case, he has, like the *pour-soi* must everywhere and always, given his own meanings and assigned his own structures to Heidegger's distinctions—has re-created them, as it were, into an altogether novel system quite unmistakably his own. I am indifferent to questions of influence here, but it will further our appreciation of Sartre's notion of our being responsible for the way the world is, to place it next to a Heideggerian concept of considerable intrinsic interest.

In *Being and Time*, Heidegger identified two distinct but complexly interrelated structures in which objects may be fitted. The first may be supposed the structure of scientific or theoretical understanding broadly construed, according to which objects are seen in terms of their causal relations with one another and as covered by laws which it is the aim of science to discover. Descriptions of objects relative to this framework, in such terms as mass and energy, temperature and velocity, metabolism and mitosis, have application to things as they presumably are in themselves and without reference to any human purpose or intervention. The scientist seeks, as it were, to describe how the world is independently of any facts connected to human understanding or description of it—to describe it in the way a detached or even a disembodied external intellect might. Many terms of ordinary discourse also belong to this mode of description: "dog," "tree," "star" are terms chosen out of many, which apply to things indifferently as to any use we might make of them, even if in fact dogs, trees, and stars also fit into practical and utilitarian contexts, and subserve human ends as instruments. Under these objective descriptions, as we may call them, objects are designated *vorhanden* by Heidegger: objects as they are, I suppose he means to imply, before they are touched by the practical hand of man. The other structure is just the one of utility and instrumentation, viewed as what Heidegger terms *zuhanden*: things as they present themselves as means through which actions may be performed and goals approached. "House" is doubtless a term from the vocabulary of *Zuhandenheit*, since it carries the meaning of shelter, although it is always possible to give a noninstrumental description, in terms say of statics, of stresses and strains, of just the objects picked out by "house." No doubt, too, its being an instrument for shelter presupposes a certain causal knowledge, but the latter fails to determine the use to which the object is put: Martians might master the physics of houses without ever learning what ends they served or even that they are means. Anything can be imagined to serve some purpose and so to fit into a structure of use, but when it does, it immediately acquires a whole set of new relationships to other things, and these things then compose systems that are otherwise independent of the relations revealed by an abstract scientific description. They *refer* to one another, Heidegger suggests, the way the hammer refers to the nail and the nail to the board, all of them forming together a kind of totality of interreferential tools—a *Zeugganzes*—which exists as a system of interlocking functions only relative to the practicalities of human contrivance.

A Cartesian spirit, one concerned to represent the world as it is independent of himself or of anyone's knowledge of it, approaches the world from the perspective of *Vorhandenheit*. A Marxist agent, concerned to change the world to fit his representations of how it should be for human occupancy, views things through the perspective of *Zuhandenheit*. The concept already encountered in our discussion of the situation is a specialization of this notion, as indeed is the immediately affiliated concept of praxis, which plays a crucial role in Sartre's later, marxified philosophy in the *Critique de la raison dialectique*. Both of these concepts have reference to systems of relationships among objects which in a way are there only by virtue of being put there through our intervention, through the practical structures of man engaged in remaking things to his own ends. Things

Engagement | 85

acquire significance, take on meaning, only so far as and because we engage with them. When we so engage with the world, its objects no longer are merely *vorhanden* or *en-soi*. They are *zuhanden* and (though Sartre does not quite use the expression) *pour-nous*.

This restructuring of things takes place prereflectively to begin with: the world is already so ordered the moment we are in it—or better, the moment we are conscious of it. There are other ways of being in the world, say as objects, as lumps of matter or protein, which do not count. It is, then, a world given a shape and contour it would not have without us, much in the way in which things cast shadows only in the presence of light. Sartre's peer, his fellow philosopher and one-time coeditor of *Les Temps Modernes,* Maurice Merleau-Ponty, makes the point in *The Phenomenology of Perception* in the following way. The phenomenal field does not present itself as so many discrete bits of experience, as a mosaic of atomistic data. It is structured, and the bits refer to and in a sense interpenetrate one another. But neither is this structure imposed from without by a kind of pure intellect assigning order to inherently unstructured flow—as Kant, or at least certain ways of reading Kant would suggest. Rather, the structures already are there, spontaneously and prereflectively synthesized, antecedently to any intellectual reorganization. Merleau-Ponty supposes this prereflective synthesis to be due to the way our bodies are structured, and he attempts to confirm this in rather massive detail by showing how various bodily defects go with what may be considered distortions (relative to the normal body) in the phenomenal field. But in any case, and much in the same way that existence is alleged to precede essence, the structuring of objects into systems precedes any conscious reflections; by the time we are aware of the structures, they are already there, as though the self and the world the self lives in were mutually interdependent poles of a single process. To be in the world is already to have modified the world into a structure of meanings which is there only because we are. It is almost as though one had to distinguish between two dimensions of objective being: between the way the world is *en-soi*, independent of any human participation, which roughly corresponds to Heidegger's *vorhanden*; and the world as it is *for us*, which even more roughly corresponds to his *zuhanden*. And it is in the latter way that the world is given to us.

We may, if we wish, use Sartre's term to make the point explicit: we may say that the moment the *pour-soi* exists it is related to the world. It has to be related to the world because it is after all just consciousness, and there is no consciousness without an object, but the world of which it is conscious is thereby *situationalized*. And the world as it is *en-soi*, as *vorhanden*, is a kind of abstract backdrop, never really given through experience, because through experience it is situationalized. So we have after all something not so remarkably different from Kant's distinction between phenomena and things-in-themselves. Merleau-Ponty argued—and the position is almost orthodox in phenomenology—that we arrive at such a conception of objects by abstracting from experience, that it is a kind of intellectual construction which we do not and cannot begin with, since it amounts to a kind of desituationalized view of the world.

It is almost moot whether such a view of the world is intelligible at all. Other philosophers, pre-eminently Marxists, have argued more strongly that we never really arrive at such a cold dehumanized world: knowledge is only and always praxis, and we know the world only situationally; this view enables one to speak not even loosely or metaphorically of the *world-of-the-bourgeoisie* or *of-the-proletariat* (I use the hyphens to register the inseparability of the world from those whose organization of it gives it, in a certain way, a kind of definition). The Sophist Protagoras is famous for having claimed that each man is the measure of things as they are for him, which was understood to entail a relativization of truth to persons who severally laid down different and mutually inscrutable worlds. In virtue of the manner in which the *pour-soi* is related to the world, this is not an altogether far-fetched view of things, though from the perspective of the world *en-soi* it is false. There is room here then for an endless debate, the historically first episode in which was doubtless the dialectical wrestle between Protagoras and Socrates over whether there is such thing as a common truth and if there is not, then how can there be anything we might remotely think of as education? And how could Protagoras at once consider himself a teacher and believe that everyone is always right—for his world?

I shall not protract these matters here: I wish only to emphasize how crucial the distinctions I have been sketching are in understanding Sartre. For when he contrasts things with our consciousness of things, when he insists, as he tirelessly does, that it is as deep a philosophical error as the wayward intellect is capable of to treat human beings not just morally but conceptually as though they were objects, it is mandatory that we recognize that he is using the latter term strictly in terms of *Vorhandenheit*. For the world as it is *for us*, organized in the light of meanings that originate in consciousness and do so before reflection occurs, has already in a way something like the structures that belong to consciousness. It has, for instance, a kind of intensional structure. For much as we hold beliefs whether or not they are true, so things have the meanings we give them whether or not it is true or even sensible to wonder whether they have those meanings as such. Presumably it does not make sense. So the world as lived—at the point of intersection between consciousness and objects, where the latter flood the former and the former situationalizes the latter—the lived world participates in both domains of being.

We may see this with a certain clarity if we recall for a moment that point which Sartre made so much of in the prefatory pages of *Being and Nothingness*: that things have inexhaustibly many aspects other than those immediately given to consciousness. It does not follow that a thing has meaning for us, or the same meaning at least, under each of its aspects. Certain aspects objectively available are irrelevant to the situation, to the thing as integrated into the system of possibilities, obstacles, opportunities, and the like which give it situational import and significance for us. Other aspects could be relevant but only in different situations, for different persons, or for us at different times. Obviously not everything, and not everything about anything, can be relevant all at once, or the whole point of relevancy falls away. So it is through the concept of relevance that the situationalized world has an intensional structure. This is part of what the notion of engagement means. Engagement contrasts with *standing apart from*, again in the posture of a disinterested Cartesian spirit for whom the concept of relevance either has no meaning or only has the meaning of intellectual relevance, and if it has *that*, then even to see the world as an intellectual is to be engaged in a thin sort of way. To be engaged, to be there (*être-là*) is pretty much a synonym for the *pour-soi* in general existentialistic thought: *Dasein*, literally "being-there," is Heidegger's term of art for designating humans.

Heidegger was never remarkably concerned with the concept of consciousness as such—his *Dasein* is simply a being cast into the world at one point rather than another, who has to find his way to an authentic existence wherever he is cast. Nothing like the tight conceptual connections between consciousness and reality were thus available to Heidegger, who in any case came increasingly to be obsessed with the yonder term in the nexus, with Being as Being, with which, he supposed, we have become more and more out of touch since the earliest days of philosophy and to which he hoped through his philosophy to lead us back. But for Sartre, the *en-soi* remains in the background, which is one reason his existentialism is a humanism: human beings are at the center of his concerns as a technical philosopher and as a person, and reference to the *en-soi* figures chiefly as a logical counterfoil for what he wants to say about man. "Subjectivity is the beginning point," and everything is supposed to develop out of a structural analysis of the *cogito*. So for Sartre, the world is pretty much *our* world, so that he can say with a kind of studied recklessness, "Without the world there is no selfness, no person; without selfness, without the person, there is no world."[1] This can be made to sound crazy: the sun and the moon, to mention but two recalcitrant entities, are part of the world but can hardly be thought to evaporate with the vanishing of persons. But in the sense in which the world is a set of meanings, rather than just a set of neutral objects—made up of facts, not things, to echo perhaps misleadingly Wittgenstein's distinction—the saying makes sense and is pos-

[1] *Being and Nothingness*, p. 104.

sibly even true. In this sense, when I go the world goes—at least *my* world does—and things are returned to a set of bare things in themselves, as they would be perhaps for God. "This quality of 'my-ness' in the world is a fugitive structure, always present, a structure which I *live*." And again: "The world (*is*) mine because it is haunted by possibles. . . . It is these possibilities which give the world its unity and meaning as the world."[2]

These reflections may enhance our grasp of a further point in Sartre's philosophy. The waiter may play at being a waiter, and he may be wrong in believing that he is a waiter only in a certain sense of identity—identification with one's role is not identity with it as spoken of by metaphysicians and logicians. But if he believes he is a prime minister or the conqueror of Spain, or a geisha girl or a crab apple, he will not be a victim so much of Bad Faith as of a kind of madness. So in a way only someone who is a waiter in a primary sense can believe he is a waiter in the philosophically damaged and psychologically damaging sense. This is perfectly general: I am a man, and so can play the roles of being a man, and think wrongly that masculinity is my essence. But still, my gender, my social and economic status, all these are thrust upon me, and I have no special options save with respect to what my postures relative to these givens are to be. These quite external matters Sartre refers to as my *facticity*: I don't choose my life as those detached spirits in the last book of Plato's *Republic* choose amongst the array of lives laid out before them, he observes. Yet even so, being born a bourgeois or whatever does not "constitute me as *being* a bourgeois,"[3] and by this I believe he means that I must

[2] *Ibid.*
[3] *Ibid.*, p. 83.

structure my life in those terms, must make them my own in giving a certain meaning to undisputed facts. The *pour-soi* "is not what it is," but neither can it escape its facticities.

This complicated thought might be given focus by thinking for a moment of feminism. Consciousness as consciousness knows no gender. But since always in the world, it must live with what it is given—as gender is, among other traits. But then being a woman does not constitute being one: one has to choose, as it were, one's femininity. At this point this sounds like a curious limitation on freedom after all, almost as though there were only the sort of freedom the Stoics and Nietzsche spoke of in connection with their concept of *amor fati*, to accept one's fate and make it one's own by internalizing it. I stand at once attached to and distant from the fatalities of my life. "Facticity," Sartre writes, "is only one indication which I give myself of the being to which I must reunite myself in order to be what I am."[4] Of course and as always, I can only be what I am "in the mode of not-being it," through the repudiating structures of nihilations, and the connections ontologically and conceptually between freedom and facticity are complex. I shall consider them again when I take up Sartre's notion of original choice. But for the present it is enough to have distinguished two senses of "world" or, as Sartre would prefer, two ways in which the world is. So considered, the problem of knowing the world calls for a special bit of analysis.

However closely world and self may be patterned on one another, there is an inevitable and uncollapsible distance between them. This distance must be under-

[4] *Ibid.*

stood as logically different from the distances to be found between things and within the world. Perhaps we can best begin to grasp it by thinking as a metaphor of *pointing* or *deixis* or, semantically speaking, of *denoting*. For the structures of nihilation are, in a manner, found in denotation. Thus, a sign stands for, and so is not, the object it picks out. An arrow points toward a target, and between it and the target, in addition to the distance, there is a direction. Nothing points to itself, so that even when we have what we might speak of as self-reference, the sign plays *two* roles, one as a pointer and the other the object pointed to, and incorporates within its structure the kind of logical distance that normally stands between indicators and their objects.

Consciousness can be regarded in these terms as well: as a kind of pointing to its objects from which it must then be logically distant. Since wherever we have deixis in this sense, we have a metaphoric space between sign and object, we can portentously speak of them as separated by a kind of "nothingness." I believe the whole high-flown apparatus of nothingness in Sartre's thought is merely a device for speaking of the distance between sign and object: consciousness is *of* an object it is distinct from, and in a way is only this of-ness; since the of-ness still has to be distinguished from the object in question, we may speak of consciousness as nothing but this difference and hence a kind of directed nothingness. To be human, or at least to be a consciousness (it is curious that Sartre always uses the terms interchangeably, as though dogs did not have consciousness or did not engage with their doggy universes!), is always to stand at a distance from the world: or perhaps just is to be this distance.

The issue becomes as complicated when we are objects for ourselves as it does for self-referential expressions: I exist as the target for a deixis as well as exist as the deixis itself, and between me as object and me as consciousness this logical distance is again incorporated. In such cases, moreover, I am within the world as object and outside the world as consciousnessness of the object; the conceptually uniting of the two calls for a remarkable piece of recognition. (Gabriel Marcel, in his *Journal métaphysique*, considers it a mystery that the two can be connected in thought at all.) The very notions of *être-là*—or *Dasein*—imply not merely a location but a deixis. The terms "here" and "now" are deictic expressions, pointing to places and times respectively cospatial and contemporary with their utterance. But more crucially for our purposes here, the concept of knowledge, in Sartre's philosophy, embodies these features. Knowledge, for Sartre, is not, or not basically anyway, construed propositionally, as knowledge that such and such is the case. Rather, it is construed as a matter of immediate acquaintance with something, a *presence-to* an object here and now. Indeed, since consciousness also is simply presence-to an object here and now, knowledge and consciousness in this sense come to the same thing. And so a distinction and a distance are always implied between the knower and that to which he is present. "Presence incloses a radical negation as presence to that which one is not."[5] Knowledge is the primordial linkage through which we are at once tethered to and sundered from the world of objects, a world which is other and alien even if (in the sense hopefully made clear in the remarks of this chapter) *mine*.

[5] *Ibid.*, p. 173.

Being present-to is not a connection in which objects can be related. Or, as Sartre knottily puts it, "The in-itself [*en-soi*] can never by itself be *presence*."[6] Things may be juxtaposed, in mutual contact, beside or above or next to one another, and they may be separated by physical distances. But presence-to the world is never a relationship within the world: it stands at right angles to whatever relationship between things may be found in the world of the *en-soi*. It involves a relationship between two quite different sorts of being, only one of which is or can be an object at all. I say "can be" deliberately, because though the self may, as we saw, be an an object, consciousness cannot be: it is always only *of* objects.

It may very well be, as Sartre argues, that knowledge as presence-to is a mode of being,[7] and indeed it hardly can be otherwise if knowledge and (reflective) consciousness are one. But it must be kept as clear as I fear I have failed to make it, that knowledge is a mode of being logically excluded from the world of objects, in which knowers as knowers can have no place: they cannot, obviously, be fused with what they know, they are in perpetual exile from any possible object of knowledge—the latter being, in Santayana's beautiful phrase, a salutation and not an embrace. To imagine there were a fusion would entail "the solidification of the for-itself in the it-self, and at the same stroke, the disappearance of the world and of the in-itself as presence."[8] So Roquentin must always stand at a distance from the chestnut root or cease being Roquentin, or at least a

[6] *Ibid.*, p. 172.
[7] *Ibid.*, p. 174.
[8] *Ibid.*, p. 178.

person. Fusion is an impossible and hopeless ideal, however mystics may long for it to happen and however romantics in epistemology may regard it as a paradigm; its victory would be its defeat, which is another element in the portrait of man as a futile passion. And since knowledge—or consciousness—is always of a world of which it forms no part, the nothingness Heidegger perceived as surrounding the world in its totality can in one respect be attributed to the nothingness that we are (remembering that nothingness is not—nothing). "The very apprehension of the world as totality causes the appearance *alongside the world* of a nothingness which sustains and encompasses this totality."[9] And this is us: *we* are the boundaries of the world, and so we are of a different order of being altogether than any boundaries which may divide the world from within. Or: we are the boundary of the revealed world[10] and the condition of its revelation.

These have been difficult paragraphs, and it is not clear that one can talk about these subjects save metaphorically or poetically, inasmuch as language is after all designed to talk about the world rather than any connection between itself and the world: and a special wrenching-free from ordinary references is required to make reference itself the subject of discourse. Wittgenstein, indeed, supposed that we could not in principle bring into language, as part of what it represents, the conditions of representation: language could *show* the world, but not the fact that it showed it; and so, regarding the semantical liaison between the two, we

[9] *Ibid.*, p. 181.

[10] At *Tractatus* 5.632, Ludwig Wittgenstein writes, "The subject does not belong to the world but it is a limit of the world."

must, he said, be silent. Much the same thing may be said about consciousness, which enhances the systematic analogies between the structures of language and of consciousness which I have been seeking to exploit. Consciousness is typically always *of* the world, and almost never *of* itself in this way. Sartre, as we have seen, supposes that we always and necessarily are conscious of being conscious, but consciousness is never in this sense given to itself the way the world is given to it: it is never an *object* for itself. And it is not clear that it *can* be an object for itself, if we think of it as a kind of absolute transparency which never penetrates the objects it is of. It is logically invisible, as it were. But then if it became an object, it would have to be visible to itself and hence could not be given to itself the way it really is, namely, as a pure transparency. But we are, obviously and with a vengeance, back once more in a form of metaphorical description.

In any case, and for whatever it may be worth, the picture we now have is of a self absolutely separate from a world it more or less monitors from without, and on which this monitoring makes no mark whatever. Something more is required if we are to effect the transition between this conception, as Cartesian as it is Sartrian, and the notion that the world is *mine*, compounded out of *my* possibilities. I must have a place in and not outside the world, if this latter structure is to apply. And the connection will be made through the concept of action: I must be knower and agent at once. And indeed I am this: Sartre writes that "knowledge and action are only two abstract aspects of an original, concrete relation."[11] So if the world is revealed through knowledge, it is structured through action. "How does it

[11] *Being and Nothingness*, p. 308.

happen," Sartre asks, "that I am not a barren, indefinitely repeated negation of the *this* as pure *this*?" How, to put it differently and, we may add, in the Heideggerian framework of *Zuhandenheit*, can instrumentality arise in the world?[12]

I can get some purchase on the problem by thinking again of qualities, though in a more sophisticated or at least existentialist way than Roquentin did in his metaphysical soliloquy. A monitoring Cartesian intelligence would merely note the qualities before it, would barrenly indicate the qualities of a thing which is just the sum of its separate qualities, each distinct from the other and united externally only through the fact that each belongs to the same thing—by the "principle of the series." But this is in fact not at all the way qualities are revealed. In a passage which says almost everything Merleau-Ponty managed to express in the whole of the *Phenomenology of Perception*, Sartre writes:

> ... The lemon is extended throughout all its qualities, and each of its qualities is extended throughout each of the others. It is the sourness of the lemon which is yellow, it is the yellow of the lemon which is sour. We eat the color of a cake, and the taste of this cake is the instrument which reveals its shape and its color to what we may call the alimentary intuition. Conversely if I poke my finger into a jar of jam, the sticky coldness of that jam is a revelation to my fingers of its sugary taste. The fluidity, the tepidity, the bluish color, the undulating restlessness of the water in a pool are given at one stroke, each quality through the others; and it is this total interpenetration which we call the *this*.[13]

[12] *Ibid.*, p. 201.
[13] *Ibid.*, p. 186.

It is a fascinating passage. Sartre implies not just that a blind man does not understand the meaning of *color* predicates—a view often held as a matter of doctrine at least since Locke and the *philosophes*—but that his understanding even of taste predicates must differ from our own, since he hardly can taste the "yellow" of the lemon in its sourness. His understanding of a term such as "lemon" itself must differ sharply from those with sight, who interact with the world through the normal repertoire of sense modalities—so much so that if Sartre were completely correct, communication with the blind ought to be impossible. The passage implies as well the role which the interventions of the body play in the constitution of the world. This, as I have mentioned, is Merleau-Ponty's basic philosophical conclusion, and inasmuch as his and Sartre's thoughts on the body are remarkably parallel, this will be as good a place as any to describe the connection between the *pour-soi* and its physiological embodiment: for after all the body seems the natural vehicle for its intersection with the world.

Though Sartre bases a tremendous amount of his philosophy on largely Cartesian structures, on the *cogito* and its logic, he clearly deviated from the Cartesian view of material objects, a point already apparent in the very idea of the world-for-us. For Descartes, bodies were mechanically or geometrically defined objects, the human body no less so than ordinary and less complex ones, and it is a serious problem for Cartesian philosophy that the connection between minds and bodies has to be a mystery or a miracle. Descartes, it is true, said in a perplexing passage in the *Meditations* that one is not in one's body the way a pilot is in a ship—or, in Ryle's later paraphrase, the way a ghost is in a machine—but this is just the way we would have expected minds to be in bodies from the principles previously laid down in that work. Indeed, there are two sorts of gap between the two: a cognitive and a causal one. The first concerns the whole problem of how one comes to know of the existence of external objects (one's own body included), it having been a problem for Descartes how we are justly to infer from the content and structure of our minds, from our representation of the world, anything certain as to how the world is or if there is a world at all. In fact, it is consistent with my representing myself as having a body, and a body of a certain sort, that I in fact have none; for the self is logically independent of any bodily substance, and I cannot, Descartes argued, be identical with my body in any case. I cannot because I am unable consistently to deny my own existence but am able to deny my body's existence: so they cannot be the same. The second problem arises in connection with Descartes's picture of the differences between minds and bodies: how in principle is a spaceless, weightless, utterly unphysical thing like a mind able to cause the movement of a spatial, crass object like a body? How, merely by intending that my arm go up, can it happen that it does? In a way, Sartre and Merleau-Ponty attempt to close both gaps at once, by a radical recharacterization of minds and bodies together, by supposing that there is just one thing which stands in that original relationship with the world of which Sartre says that action and knowledge are but two abstract limits. And the gist of this view is that I *am* my body.[14] But of course the concept of the body has to be freshly thought out.

Consider, for example, my hand. With my hand,

[14] *Ibid.*, p. 323.

which moves a stick, I move a stone. Hand, stick, and stone together constitute an instrumental whole, each "referring" to the other after the manner of a *Zeugganzes*. But to what anterior thing if any does the *hand* refer? The traditional philosophical answer might have been: to the mind, to an act of will, or some such thing. But Sartre states that the hand, in this instance, "is the arresting of references and their ultimate end." The body, generally speaking, is the center of the world for me, that to which everything refers back but which itself refers back to nothing. Sartre says it is "at once the unknowable and non-utilizable term which the last instrument of the series indicates."[15] This may sound puzzling, but its intent is clear. It is not known because it is not an object of knowledge but the very fact of knowledge. And it is not used because it is the very fact of using (and to suppose that it is used would require something distinct, which used it, and this sends us back into an infinite regression). Marcel, in the concluding pages of his *Journal métaphysique*, dwells originally and impressively on these matters, and whatever may have been his influence on Sartre, he epitomizes Sartre's thought in saying, "I do not *use* my body: I *am* my body."[16] So in the sense in which a stick is a tool, my hand is not a tool. And in the sense in which the stick might be an object of knowledge, my knowing the stick is not, except perhaps prereflectively. Between myself and my body no gap has to be traversed by cognition or causation. Merleau-Ponty writes, "The union of soul and body is not an amalgamation between two mutually external terms, subject and object, brought

[15] *Ibid.*

[16] Gabriel Marcel, *Journal métaphysique* (Paris, 1927), p. 323.

about by arbitrary decree. It is enacted at every instant in the movement of existence. . . . We have found underneath the objective and detached knowledge of the body that other knowledge which we have of it in virtue of its always being with us and of the fact that we are our body." And Merleau-Ponty concurs as well with Sartre's conception of knowledge: "My body is not an object," he concludes.[17]

Once more, of course, my body or parts of it may be objects, as when one contemplates his navel, or when an infant examines his hand as an odd, alien object on a level with the rattle to which it is attached. But this is not the typical or central relationship in which one stands to one's body: one does not know it, one *lives* it. So, finally, in thinking that one's knowledge of one's body is representationalistic, Descartes quite totally misconceived it, himself, and his relationship to it, creating muddles which three centuries of philosophy had tried to unravel, when the correct solution is the radical one: to show that the muddle ought never to have come up at all, to show that it is due, as Merleau-Ponty thought, to the misapplication of a form of description which has valid application elsewhere, namely, the objective or scientific picture of knowledge—a categorial confusion of *vorhanden* and *zuhanden*, roughly speaking. The scientific picture views my body from the outside, so to speak, and though the success of physiology demonstrates that it can be viewed that way, this is not the primordial way of viewing: the body is quite different for anatomists and lovers. Sartre writes in a summary way, "Being-for-itself must be wholly body and it must

[17] Maurice Merleau-Ponty, *The Phenomenology of Perception*, trans. Colin Smith (New York, 1962), pp. 88–89, 206, 198.

be wholly consciousness: it can not be *united* with the body."[18] It cannot because only what is first separate can be united, and the burden of this novel analysis has been to abort any such sundering. "In fact what I am cannot on principle be an object for me inasmuch as I am *it*."[19]

I am far from certain that this analysis can indeed do whatever it is intended to do, and it will have serious problems in accounting for both errors in cognition and misperformances in action, but exploitation of these questions would carry us irresponsibly beyond our expository aims. So, returning to the interreferential system which is our world, a world in which objects are united through the ligature of meanings one gives it, Sartre proposes this: "These references could not be grasped by a purely contemplative consciousness. For such a consciousness the hammer would not refer to the nails but would be alongside them; furthermore the expression 'alongside' loses all meaning if it does not outline a path which goes from the hammer to the nail. . . ." Thus, "the world from the moment of the upsurge of my For-itself is revealed as the indication of acts to be performed."[20] In a way, the structure of the "lived world" gives the solution to the problem. If I were just a disengaged consciousness, the world would not have the structure I see it to have, it would appear incommensurately different. We do not survey the world, but rather are engaged in it.[21] We can put this somewhat differently. If I suppose myself withdrawn from the world, so that it lies before me as a kind of ob-

[18] *Being and Nothingness*, p. 305.
[19] *Ibid.*, p. 318.
[20] *Ibid.*, pp. 321–22.
[21] *Ibid.*, p. 327.

jective landscape, it has no center, so to speak, though I may pay attention to one bit of it rather than to another. But the structure of the lived world has a center from which paths of action radiate out or to which they all at last lead back. And that center, which itself has no center, is me.

We have worked our way through a number of very closely connected characterizations of the *pour-soi*. It is consciousness, it is also a sort of nothingness, it is also freedom and also anguish. And, as we have just seen, it is body also. On each of these aspects Sartre writes densely and imaginatively, in detail and with an acuity that only the reader of *Being and Nothingness* itself can appreciate. But there is a further critical dimension, namely, temporality, on which we have already touched but which demands a further gloss before we conclude this discussion.

In one formulation, the *pour-soi* is "present-to" the world. But "present" has, in French as in English, a temporal as well as a confrontational meaning, the present being *now*. The *pour-soi*, for all its spontaneity, is not merely a staccato of succeeding "nows"—if it were always only conscious of the present, it would have no consciousness of presentness or of time at all—and here is one case in which the $F(c)=c(F)$ formula yields a striking result: the consciousness of temporality entails the temporality of consciousness. There is a continuity to be accounted for, but it is a complex one in Sartre's theory, and I shall now try to work it out. To begin with, the presentness of consciousness is the consciousness of presentness. But "present" has meaning only with conceptual reference to "was" and "will be," temporal distinctions standing in mutual conceptual coimplication. The structure entails a kind of historical location.

But, as we saw, one's consciousness of a moment ago is gone: one is united with it only through not being it (any longer)—as with the gambler. In nihilating whatever is the object to which I am present, I simultaneously nihilate the consciousness that I was. But one feels these two sorts of nihilation have to be distinguished in some way: when I nihilate the object, I am not it *tout court*, and it is not me; yet when I nihilate my past, I am one with it, albeit, as Sartre enjoys saying, in the mode of not being it. In any case, the important dimension in this analysis is the future. Symmetrically with my past, I am my future in the mode of not being it (as yet); it is what I will be but am not now. This is not a mere abstract consequence of the concept of temporal order. I experience the world as having meanings for me, and this is to experience it as the arena of possible actions, which are referred to my future. Or, to put it in another way, to perceive the world as a scene of action is to see it as characterized by certain *lacks* which may be removed by action, and these refer me to the future. Of course, when the future arrives, the present will be perceived again as lacking, and this goes on and on. And these lacks, insofar as they are objective, give the world a future as well as giving it to me.

One never reaches a point where the world goes utterly solid, where there are no lacks—not unless one withdraws from it, and this, as the *Gita* says of "body-bearing souls," is not a possibility. Sartre speaks of this movement from lack to lack as a "perpetual flight," and while we may interpret this statement variously, the point of it is to tie one more ontological knot between the structure of the self and the structure of his world: the self's temporality is the world's. Sartre, as usual, is inclined to construe things gloomily. He feels that we are somehow frustrated by the fact that we can never become one with our future, whatever this may be, or "reunited" with ourselves.[22] Of course, we also cannot be united with someone else or, for that matter, with an object. But these are abstract matters, and external, not defining traits of the self the way temporality is. The gloom is due to the fact that we aspire to a kind of solidity—temporal solidity might just be timelessness—which it is not in our nature to achieve. In any case, there is no escape from temporality any more than there is from freedom, so long as we exist at all.

It has been remarked by some philosophers that the concepts of altruism and prudence are very closely related. For it is not clear that I can have any more grounded an obligation to a future self (me) than to an other self (say, you): or if I do have the first, a basis has already been established for the second. I am no more and no less separated from my future self than from contempary other selves. So much has been argued by Henry Sidgwick, and more recently by the American moralist Thomas Nagel. It is, I think, a parity which Sartre would deny. I stand, after all, in a somewhat more intimate relationship with my future self than with other selves. It is *my* future, after all, insofar as temporality is a structure of consciousness. I *am* my future, even if in the mode of not being it. But, as we just argued, I do not have this intimacy of liaison with objects or for that matter with others. So the analogy between prudence and altruism is rather dubious.

We shall take up the logic of our relations with others in a moment. But a word more must be said on the notion of the *pour-soi* as its "own lack." Through this feature of consciousness, the world is itself constituted as "lacking" and thus as an instrumental complex. It

[22] *Ibid.*, p. 202.

will be an easy transition from this concept to that of praxis, which is the central cognitive category of Sartre's *Critique de la raison dialectique*, fusing as it does the aspects of knowledge and action at once, much as it is an easy transition from the concept of lack to that of *need*, which is in a way a modulation of the same concept in a Marxian key. And the entire complex can be given a kind of Stakhanovite reading: to be conscious is to have work to do, a condition imposed upon us through the structure of our being, and not just a kind of punishment such as the sons of Adam endure, having to earn their bread in the sweat of their brows—unless just being consciousnesses is a kind of punishment, and the separation from the world of things a kind of fall. Knower and agent at once, I am interlocked with a world whose shape and meaning are given by me. Against this background we must now attempt to understand the conceptual difficulties which arise from the logically unforeseeable obstrusion of other persons—a matter I have referred to far too casually so far. A whole new structure is needed to accommodate the recognition that they have a special sort of existence for me and I for them which mere objects have for neither of us and certainly not for one another. On this topic Sartre says some of his most interesting and original things, and it deserves a chapter of its own.

Shame: or, the Problem of Other Minds

# IV

Toward the end of *No Exit*, Sartre's most original if not his finest play, when the situation in which they are locked has become rudely clear to the three occupants of a room in hell, the male character, Garcin, voices what must be Sartre's most famous phrase: *"L'enfer c'est les autres."* Hell is "other people" in the respect that each of these personages is trapped eternally in moral and erotic impasses from which none is able to allow any of the others to escape. The basis of their spiritual torment lies deeper, however, than their diabolically mismatched psyches imply (mismatched save for the purposes of inflicting agony upon one another, that is: for *that* purpose they are fiendishly matched). Each demands that he or she be taken at the value he or she would want to be taken, that others perceive him as they would want to perceive themselves; because there is a mutual refusal, indeed incapacity to do this, each is forced to see himself through the eyes of the others, and none can escape an identity imposed from without. Each sees the acts of the others in the harshest possible light, and since these acts sum up their several lives, and since each is dead, none can by any further act redeem his life from these chill and fatal assessments; the lives are all played out. And so, by a cruel cunning, the stalemated fellowship in this banal and so all-the-more-hideous chamber—so different from what the mythology of hell has taught those who fear it to expect—is composed of persons who are exactly suited to be one another's psychic torturer; instead of a pit of flames and pincers, hell is a hopeless conversation in which the soul of each is ruthlessly exposed and the identity of each is hostage to his spiritual captors—none breaks free from a circular dialogue turning forever about the same dead center.

But *No Exit*, which is perhaps the most remarkable literary embodiment of a philosophical idea ever written, is meant to have a universal application, and the architectures of cruelty so vividly exhibited by the rather despicable inmates—each of whom in his life had betrayed others and certainly caused suffering enough to merit a moral penalty in hell, each of whom was morally weak and deeply selfish—are precisely meant to exemplify the human condition everywhere and always, even as lived by saints and moral heroes, certainly by you and me. Hell is other people just because they are people and other, and the saying does not have reference only to the commonplace recognition that people vex and frustrate one another, drag one another down as in bad marriages or unhappy families or thwarted enterprises where the needed cooperations are not forthcoming. For there are happy marriages and happy families too, as well as successful common undertakings in

## Shame: or, the Problem of Other Minds | 109

which individuals function marvelously as members of a team. Even in these, however, "Hell is other people" is applicable and applies; the structures it is meant to epitomize are just the structures in which we are related to others, however benignly. From these structures there is no exit, and the dividing line between hell and ordinary daily life is not there to be drawn; other people are hell in and out of any specific inferno. The practices and feelings which might commonly be believed to provide avenues of escape—love, trust, charity, friendship, and the like—are, in Sartre's corrosive and deflationist argument, examples of the disease it is an illusion to suppose instead they might cure, examples rather than counter-examples, all the more cruel because they seem to be counter-examples to the general case they in fact illustrate. Like all of Sartre's slogans, this one condenses philosophical theories of the most extraordinary scope and subtlety, and illustrates in the darkest colors a thesis in ontology and epistemology, a concept which can be framed and phrased in the tight thin idiom of pure philosophy. It would, of course, not be Sartre were there not this double vocabulary and dual mode of presentation: the art gives life to the philosophy, and the philosophy structure to the art. But nowhere more than in this topic must the reader keep his philosophical bearings, for only so can he judge the suitability of the illustrations. I shall accordingly devote this chapter to the subject of our relations with others, analyzed in Part Three of *Being and Nothingness*, where Sartre introduces an ontologically primitive kind of being to complete his inventory of the posits of consciousness: *être-pour-autrui*, or being-for-others.

Let us recall a basic logical feature of those propositions by means of which we describe mental states, or ascribe mental states to persons. These are irreducibly intensional, in the respect that fear, for example, or desire or belief or hope or whatever, have objects: Garcin fears death, Inez desires Estelle and believes that Garcin is a coward, Estelle hopes that she is attractive to Garcin, and so on. There may, as we saw, be exceptions. There may be states of anxiety having no specific objects which, because of this, will be contrasted with specialized anxieties (over one's job, one's sexual abilities, or the like): their object, if any, is life itself, or the world at large. Or again, in contrast with happiness *that*, or depression *over*, there may be objectless states of euphoria or dejection. But let us stick with the clearly intensional cases. If a man fears something, say a snake, he also believes that what he fears exists—for what otherwise is there to be afraid of?—and that it is threatening. (I shall disregard cases in which a drug might induce phobic states in which a man is caused to fear things he has enough cognitive sobriety left to recognize are not really threatening at all.) Someone like Descartes who held serious doubts about the external world would have to regard all such fears as logically groundless, since he also must believe that nothing answers to their purported objects—though his vagabond mind might persist in fearing what his philosophically instructed intelligence dismisses as epistemological fantasies. But this sort of disparity can exist only because the mind is insufficiently disciplined by reason. Again, to believe that $p$ is, is not *just* to be in a certain state, it is to believe that the world itself is in a certain state if the belief is about the world: namely, the state that makes the belief a true one. For to believe that $p$ is, is to believe that $p$ is true or at least to be committed to this; and again a Cartesian who had what he

## Shame: or, the Problem of Other Minds | 111

regarded as rational grounds for doubting the reality of the world would have to give up any lower-order beliefs he might have about it—though once more there might be problems in disciplining his mind to bring his propensities for believing into conformity with his philosophical intuition. But the point is in any case quite general: that mental states refer those who are in them to objects which exist, or which at least they are committed to believe exist, externally to those states: and the mental states then cannot rationally survive recognition that no such objects are there. Moreover, certain sorts of object are such that if I did not believe in their existence, I could not be in the mental states which presuppose them. Consider, in this light, the state of *shame*. Some sort of objectless shame may exist, but commonly the structure of shame is this: one feels shame *before* someone because of something one is or one has done—before God, or one's parents, or someone whose moral perceptions one respects and whose good opinion somehow matters. Of course there may be no such person. One may really be alone in the universe. An ashamed solipsist would be an odd case. Still, to feel shame is to be committed to the belief that one is not alone, the existence of others as a structure of one's consciousness being built into the very concept. The feeling of shame before God, for example, could hardly survive, save as a mental aberration and a conceptual impurity, the conversion to atheism. Discounting the special case of shame before oneself, say because one has not lived up to one's expectations or ideals, the structure of shame is such that one who had no concept of other persons could not sensibly be supposed to feel shame; the feeling simply cannot arise except with reference to other persons. The question before us is how the concept of another person, an alien consciousness, gets introduced into our conceptual scheme. (Shame, of course, is only one example of a mental state whose content requires the person to have this conceptual structure: jealousy, gratitude, condescension are others, and there are many, many more.) Reference to others arises from *within*.

Since Descartes at least, the existence of other minds has been a treacherous topic in epistemology. Passersby, he proposed, might for all one knew be intricately engineered robots, mere ambulating machines. He might have gone further: minute examination of the behavior or structure of these cloaked and hatted beings might leave me as uncertain of their personhood as my first glance at them from my window; I *judge* that they are persons but do not observe that they are, for my observations might be true and the judgment false, and how am I to know whether it is false or true? It is always, then, a skeptical possibility undetermined by external scrutiny that they have no *interiors*, which is to say, no awareness or consciousness at all. Of the fact that *I* am conscious my consciousness assures me at every instant because I am prereflectively conscious of it. But the consciousness of which I am in this way conscious is always in the nature of the case my own. So neither by this avenue nor by that of observation can the doubt once planted be removed. And even if the problem of the external world is solved, so that I can say with surety that there are things, the solution does not entail that some among these things are conscious. A whole extra apparatus is required for this, and what can its logic be?

These are questions for knowledge, it may be said, not for understanding. And one can argue this way: I must at least have the concept of an other consciousness if the doubt regarding the existence of other consciousnesses can intelligibly be raised. The question then concerns the provenance of this concept. The *pour-soi*, situated in and giving by his presence a situational structure to his world, need not ever have situationalized it to take others into account. He may be utterly alone, a kind of Crusoe insularly stranded in existence. Still, he hardly can conceive of himself as alone without the concept of company, and perhaps he could not so much as rise to a concept of *himself as himself* if he did not have this further notion. After all, he might merely have been conscious of the world and of himself after the manner of the teaching in the *Transcendence of the Ego*—as an object amongst objects having no specially intimate relationship to the one who is conscious of all this; that he is conscious might never have been raised to the levels of reflective awareness. My connection through consciousness with these various objects is not a further object, so it need never intrude upon the outwardly directed consciousness filled to logical satiety with the objects of the world. I could give a complete enumeration of the objects of my world without including, as a further entry, this fact of being conscious of them. And the way in which consciousness is self-aware, on Sartre's account, cannot turn the trick. So a person might live his whole life out in this way, never once thinking that it was a *person, himself,* that was doing all this, and so of an ontologically distinct order with reference to the furnishings of his world.

Nietzsche, in a marvelously speculative passage, asks what might be the origin of consciousness,[1] not as a matter of physiology but as something which is present to itself as consciousness, however it becomes that; and

---

[1] Friedrich Nietzsche, *The Gay Science*, V.

he asks what in the end could be the function of this further datum for consciousness, which is itself. He raises the question of its use deliberately, asking in a way what might be lost if it were lost. And the answer he gives is that in a way nothing would be lost: coming to an awareness of awareness adds no new objects, any more than learning that one sees adds special visibilia to the perceptual field, since one does not *see* that one sees. Yet something is after all added, since Nietzsche believed that consciousness has social, not to say linguistic, origins: I am thrust into position to refer to myself only through recognizing that I am the one to which others refer when they refer to me. And the advent of all this is a matter not so much of mastering some special vocabulary as of mastering a complex referential system through which a vocabulary is applied to the world, myself as a self included. There are, after all, languages without pronouns and perhaps even languages whose verbs do not conjugate into first- and third-person cases or do not conjugate in any way. But the "I," or whatever its referential equivalent might be, is co-implicated with the "you" and indeed with "he"—I master the ability to describe myself, knowing it is myself that is being described, *just* when I recognize concurrently that I am the object of description for others. This interreferential structure is needed, for after all a person could master a language of sorts without getting the notion of himself: there would just be objects (including the object which was him but which he did not specially recognize to be him), that emitted signals to one another and by so doing modified one another's behavior in a manner not remarkably different from the way they modify it by contact; even his feelings would be "out there." But, as we have seen in connection with

*Shame: or, the Problem of Other Minds* | 115

the example of shame, shame could not under the circumstances be amongst them.

Sartre's thought on these matters is not utterly different from the following. My consciousness of myself is interlocked with my consciousness of others, and specifically with their consciousness of me: to be seriously aware of myself as subject presupposes an awareness of others' awareness of me as an object. Or better: *I exist for myself* at the level of self-consciousness just and only just when I become aware of existing for others. I wish to stress the *for myself* in this phrase: it is not the respect in which consciousness is *pour-soi* at the level of prereflectivity. For it might have existed for itself in *that* way without ever attaining to this fresh perspective on its being. These remarks help, too, in explaining Sartre's notion that my body, so far as I *live* it, is unknown and unknowable to me. Since I am my body, I arrive at bodily self-consciousness only when I have the concept of my body as it is for others. "To study the way in which my body appears to the Other or the way in which the Other's body appears to me amounts to the same thing. . . . The structures of my being-for-the-Other are identical to those of the Other's being-for-me."[2] So I acquire the status of a person only when others do. Once more, I must emphasize that there may not be other persons: I may be the only consciousness there is. Still, the concept of myself, having being as a person for myself, entails an understanding of my existing for others, as the concept of an exterior presupposes the concept of an interior, so that I cannot speak of others as having only exteriors without making room in the very description for their having an interior as

---

[2] *Being and Nothingness*, p. 339.

well. As a conceptual truth, inside and outside function as conjugate notions, but equally, I think, there is no concept of myself as interior without a concept of myself as exterior, and to attain this sort of conceptual awareness in my own case immediately extends to others. Before I was conscious of others and so of myself in this internally complicated manner, I could not have described the objects in the phenomenal field as *merely* having exteriors. Though in one sense no new things may be added, to respond to the query I raised in considering Nietzsche, the things already there enter into very different relationships and acquire under this new mode of description remarkably different structures than any I would believe them to have had without this insight.

I have made a great deal here of the distinction between understanding and knowledge, between conceptual entailment and epistemic truth. For it is one thing to insist that the concept of an other consciousness is required by the application of certain descriptions to myself, and quite another matter to say that this in any way entails that others exist. It may very well be true that a man might have no sense of sin if he were innocent of the concept of God and of human disobedience, for these are interrelated notions. But we cannot argue from the fact that there are men who live with a sense of sin that God exists or that Adam disobeyed him—or we should find a proof of God's existence in any Baptist sanctuary. Sartre's altogether brilliant analysis of the self as having a being-for-others as a precondition for having consciousness of being-for-himself and others as being-for-him, does not deliver him from "the reef of solipsism." So far as solipsism demands that the existence of others be demonstrated as a condition for vanishing away, solipsism is with us for the duration, for no such demonstration is to be had. Sartre's thought can give us a demonstration at best only if taken in conjunction with a certain theory of how concepts *must* be acquired: that is, with a certain theory of learning.

There are theories, of course, and classical empiricism is an example, according to which my *basic* concepts at least are caused by some immediate sense-experience, so that if my history lacks the requisite encounter with experience, my repertoire of basic concepts is correspondingly limited. But in the first place it is questionable whether I experience individuals as conscious in anything like the way I experience apples as red—if I did, the Problem of Other Minds would be solved at a stroke. And in the second place all such theories of learning are empirical and contingent, and so cannot furnish a demonstrative support for any conceptual truth. Conceptual analysis yields only truths about concepts, not truths about the world unless the world corresponds to our concepts; and something more than conceptual analysis is required to establish such a correspondence. If there is a truth in philosophy at all, it is this: that one cannot deduce from concepts alone anything about how the world in fact is; one can only deduce how it *must* be, given certain conditions, which cannot be deduced from concepts alone. It is this which in the end renders the Ontological Argument untenable. Sartre admires certain audacious attempts by philosophers like Husserl to find "at the very heart of consciousness a fundamental, transcending connection with the other which would be constitutive of each consciousness in its upsurge,[3] and Sartre's is just that sort of attempt. But all such endeavors are based on a quite

[3] *Ibid.*, p. 233.

mistaken belief that conceptual analysis can furnish factual truths, and that bare understanding alone can be cashed in for knowledge. So in the end his enterprise is intended less to solve than to bypass the epistemological problem of other minds by insisting that the problem really is an ontological one: that one could not exist as a consciousness reflectively aware of itself unless one also existed for others. But I am insisting that one could exist "for others" in the required way—which is to say, have an exterior and perceive oneself as from without—even if there were not (and certainly without its following that there are) others for whom in fact one exists. Still, the essential and quite brilliant point remains that the emergence of a consciousness of others is of a logically different order than a consciousness of mere objects, entailing as it does a transformation of consciousness of self; entailing a loss of naïveté and of un-self-aware aloneness.

Let us now return to the structures of "my world." The *pour-soi* is, we may recall, the center of reference for the complex system of *meaningful* objects which compose it. The center, we may also recall, is not part of the field whose structure refers back to it. Or better, the body is my point of view on the world, but points of view are themselves not perceived: "The body is, in fact, the point of view on which I can take no point of view."[4] Now I am in a park, that scene of so many Sartrian discoveries. There are benches to sit on if I wish to use them, flower beds to avoid, trees to shade me, and the rest. A man sits on one of the benches. Now is he just another item in "my world," the way, say, the ornamental statue of Neptune spewing water in the fountain before

[4] *Ibid.*, p. 340.

## Shame: or, the Problem of Other Minds | 119

me? Then, Sartre writes, "his relationship with the other objects would be of the purely additive type,"[5] one more thing. But in fact to perceive him *as a man* is to perceive the whole field in a quite different way: things organize about *him* in a manner structurally like the way in which they so far have organized themselves about me. So, in a way, I get the concept of "my world" only when I get the concept of "his world." Obviously, this is not in any sense a physical change: the objects have all the same physical properties as before and sustain between themselves all the same geometrical relationships—and all of this invariant to this total transformation of the field's organization. But in recognizing him as a consciousness, "instead of a grouping *toward me* of the objects, there is now an orientation *which flees from me*."[6] It is as though the man had stolen my world by making it his. Of course, were I to discover that it was not a man there after all but merely a dummy of some sort of quirky shadow, the world would once more revert to having me as its only center, and he would be just another additive object in it. As it stands, however, another center has appeared, with the effect of negating my center—or me—by drawing me into the world as an object for him. Or so Sartre says. My world, of which I as its center am not a proper part, is taken from me and I am reduced to an object become a proper part of the world of another. Of course, it should follow that the same thing happens when he perceives *me* as a consciousness rather than a stolid entity like a statue. At this point, accordingly, a kind of logical drama begins, in which there is a spontaneous struggle for centrality and for ownership of worlds: as though I could get my

---

[5] *Ibid.*, p. 254.
[6] *Ibid.*

world back as mine only if I can reduce him to an object in it, and he likewise with me, as though there could not be room for two foci in a single world. When the park exists for him, it immediately acquires an aspect it cannot have for me and at the same time acquires an aspect I would not otherwise know about. Something always escapes me—namely, that aspect which things have for him.

The concept of reality in Sartre, as we earlier observed, is that of things having aspects not immediately given to consciousness of them: one is aware of their having aspects beyond what one perceives. But here a new *sort* of aspect altogether is revealed, one which cannot in principle be given to me, namely, the world as it is for an other will always be logically hidden to me. But of course these are not physical aspects but, rather, meanings: things have for him the meanings he gives them, and these will differ from mine just from the fact that they are given by him. The drama, then, is one in which I seek to reclaim the world as mine by reducing him to an object, a somewhat hopeless project in view of the fact that it presupposes that what I seek to objectivize is a consciousness and not an object. So the world is never going to be the same again. In any case, this recognition of another consciousness, and its recognition of me, is the conceptual translation of the literary *mot* "Hell is other people," and it is the basis, in Sartre's curiously morbid psychology, of *all* my relations with others: I shall always seek to make objects of them and they of me. And all of us shall fail.

Let us note before anatomizing these relations further that even if I should have discovered that it was not a man but a dummy—a scarecrow, say—the game is already lost. This is because the very possibility of an other consciousness is an absolute boundary on my world and

## Shame: or, the Problem of Other Minds | 121

thus a limitation on me. For in a way, one might say, until I had the concept of a world-for-an-other, I did not have really the concept of a world-for-me. What I now see to have been my world had heretofore been regarded by me as *the* world. Moreover, until now I did not perceive myself as having a location in a world at all, being logically outside it looking in. I was not an object for myself. But I have become just that by recognizing that I am, or at least can be, an object for an other. This is achieved through the concept of the look.

Sartre's discussion of looks is stunningly original. To see someone as looking at me is not just to see his eyes. For eyes as eyes are but further objects in the field, like the dead eyes in the *têtes de veau* at the butcher, things I might study and learn the physiology of without ever understanding from within that eyes can see. But in perceiving an eye as looking, I perceive myself as a possible object for that look: I lose my transparency, as it were, and become opaque even for myself. The transformation in perception in which an eye becomes a thing that looks goes together with a transformation in self-perception as well. But the point is quite general, and to perceive a look need not entail seeing someone's eyes. Walking through a village or a deserted landscape, I can get the sense that someone is looking at me though I see no one, and so no one who is seeing: and this is quite enough for me to achieve a sense of my objecthood. Sartre gives an example, now quite famous, of a voyeur peering through a keyhole. He is aware only of the keyhole and what is to be seen through it, when the sudden sound of footsteps in the corridor precipitates him into objectivity; instead of just observing a forbidden scene through a secret aperture, he is abruptly made conscious of a man, himself, peering at a forbidden scene through a keyhole—his world has expanded to include himself. Sartre restates the matter in his own terms: ". . . I have my foundation outside myself. I am for myself only as I am a pure reference to the Other."[7]

Needless to say, the voyeur will feel shame, having been caught in a compromising posture. At least he will if he is a voyeur, having internalized the conventions of privacy and the institutionalization of rights to privacy which he is violating—someone from another planet or even another culture would not necessarily be ashamed of looking through a keyhole, which is just a convenient opening. Sartre is curiously insensitive here, as elsewhere, to what we might term institutional facts, though he makes an effort, later, in the *Critique de la raison dialectique*, to introduce social concepts into the structure of consciousness. It is a failing to which he is oblivious here and, more damagingly, in his discussion of values. But shame, for Sartre, has a technical meaning considerably wider than the moral sentiment that passes under that name, and that the voyeur feels or should feel. This is one of those cases where the philosophical structure takes on a misleading coloration from the example used to illustrate it, for in the end what shame comes to is a metaphysical rather than a moral feeling. "I can be ashamed only as my freedom escapes me in order to become a given object," he writes. "The Other's look makes me be beyond my being in this world and puts me in the midst of the world which is at once *this* world and beyond this world."[8] But this would be a true philosophical characterization, if it is true at all, whatever act I were observed to perform: helping a child, saving a drowning

[7] *Ibid.*, p. 260.
[8] *Ibid.*, p. 261.

## Shame: or, the Problem of Other Minds | 123

man, battling to save the city—or eating plums, reading *Le Monde*, walking the dog: largely neutral acts all.

So we must divest shame of the moral overtones lent it by the example of the voyeur if we are to understand how its concept really functions in Sartre's philosophy. And how it functions is as follows: the content of shame is that I am an *object* and constituted as such by the other. I exist for him and even for myself as I exist for others, rather than as a pure spontaneity who "is not what it is." And as an object I depend in an ontological way upon a consciousness other than my own. The shame, in effect, concerns my solidification as an object of consciousness, and a loss or seeming loss of freedom. "I am somebody rather than nobody. I have acquired an identity I have not given myself." In the end, it is not just the way in which I might be for another consciousness that induces shame: it is, rather, the fact that I have the kind of existence that can appear to another consciousness, however it may do so.

It should be clear from this that the discovery of bad faith itself presupposes the discovery of my exteriority. I can take myself to be a waiter only insofar as I exist or can exist for others as a waiter. But to the degree that I exist as a waiter *for them* (or even for myself, in taking an external viewpoint), my freedom and identity are captive to the freedom and identity of the other. What each of us aims at—what it is our nature as humans to aim at always—is to be the "foundation" of our own being; and here we discover that our foundation lies in the freedom of another. The degradation, if it is that, is, accordingly, metaphysical rather than moral. "*I am no longer master of the situation*," as Sartre says,[9] giving a banal phrase a remarkable phil-

[9] *Ibid.*, p. 265.

osophical weight. One may, then, describe this as shame. But it is shame which is shared by everyone who has the concept of the other, and has nothing to do with any special act we perform or way we happen to be, and indeed it need not be felt as shame at all. It could even be felt as pride, the feeling one has when one believes one is seen at one's best, doing some marvelous, noble deed. To be sure, I can never guarantee that others will perceive me as I would want to be perceived, but shame in this generalized sense concerns the fact that they can perceive me at all. And in any case if there is a *feeling* of shame which exactly should correspond to the way Sartre has characterized it, this will be had only by someone who has internalized Sartre's philosophy. It is moot whether anyone who is merely conscious of others will spontaneously exemplify the Sartrian structures.

Sartre has arrived at a sort of dualism, only weakly parallel to the familiar dualism of mind and body associated with Descartes. For mind and body are logically distinct and perhaps causally independent entities, whereas the structure of consciousness and objecthood—Sartre's dualism—is much more complex. I am an object for my own consciousness only through my having become conscious of others' consciousness of me. Others cannot then be *merely* objects for my consciousness or I would not become an object for myself. The structure of self-consciousness, then, is logically social, but since I finally am an object for myself only through the provenance of other's perception of me, what I am (as an object) depends upon others and not upon myself. And this is why they are hell: my identity, even for myself, depends finally upon them. And so, as Sartre assesses the situation, I can only achieve the autonomy I seek by dominating them (and

## Shame: or, the Problem of Other Minds | 125

conversely, of course). And I cannot achieve this, since at least the concept of the other always intervenes between my consciousness of myself and myself.

We are in any case now in a position to describe what are in general our concrete relationships with others, hence ultimately the interpenetrating desperations of the *dramatis personae* of *No Exit*, which have as their common logical core the structures we have just described, however morbidly embellished. They are all, and there can be no exception in any human relationship, doomed attempts to escape from structures we can neither endure nor overcome. The pages in which these relations are exhibited through a series of dramatic and depressing scenarios, are among the most powerful and psychologically rich pages to be found in Sartre's or anyone's writing. The insight into human practices, apart from the ontological armatures which they simultaneously illustrate, are saddening and deep. They have at every point the ring of human truth, even if the philosophical analyses behind them are haywire and perverse. Sartre's discussion bears comparison with Spinoza's deduction of the modalities of passion in Book Four of the *Ethics*, where the logical derivation is a kind of *tour de force* but where the penetration into the hopelessness of the human psyche is independent of that, even if an extra appreciation is attained if it indeed can be shown that our private flaps and failings are part of the cosmic order, and inevitable. In each case Sartre takes up, whether of love or brutalization, the attempt is to capture the consciousness of an other by making the other an object. When he is an object, I get my freedom back because I am not an object for him any longer, since nothing is an object for an object. I thus disarm that consciousness from a reciprocal disarming of mine. "While I attempt to free myself from the hold of the Other, the Other is trying to free himself from mine; while I seek to enslave the Other, the Other seeks to enslave me." I am never successful in this, and I cannot be. But there is no resting place and no shrugging off the effort to repeat the effort. It is, to pre-empt a phrase of Hobbes, a restless striving for power after power which ceaseth only in death. "Conflict," Sartre goes on, "is the original meaning of being-for-others."[10] Let us show how this works in love, and the circle of attitudes it generates. "Love must always end in sorrow," runs the song in *O Lucky Man*, "and everyone must play the game."

The paradigm of love in Sartre's vision of it is Marcel's unhappy pursuit of Albertine in Proust's novel, though it could as easily be Swann's unhappy pursuit of Odette. Jealousy is its spring and motive, and Marcel seeks virtually to enslave Albertine, making her as absolutely dependent upon him as is possible and in every possible way. What he cannot capture is her consciousness or, hence, her freedom: "Through her consciousness Albertine escapes Marcel even when he is at her side."[11] Marcel, to be sure, is concerned to own her not as a thing but as a consciousness: "He wants to possess a freedom." And the strategy into which he falls is this: to become in a way the beloved's *whole world*, the sole object of her consciousness. So he consents in a way to being an object for her, anchoring in this way the fickle awareness of the beloved toward him, fastening it down. I must in a certain way conceal my freedom, enslave myself, as it were, in order to enslave her; I cannot treat her as an object, for when I do so her subjectivity or freedom disappears, and since it is

[10] *Ibid.*, p. 364.
[11] *Ibid.*, p. 366.

just this that I want, the enterprise would fail. Speaking figuratively, I must avoid looking at her.

And now suppose this strategy succeeds, and the beloved becomes a lover in her own right, in love with me. Surely this is what I thought I wanted. But what now happens is that, like me before, she seeks to become *my* whole world, enslaving herself in order to enslave me, and so to possess my freedom as I sought to possess hers, by *concealing* her freedom. If I succeed, I fail, since her freedom escapes me; there is no balance point in the affair. "To love," Sartre writes, "is to want to be loved." This is reciprocal and foredoomed, inasmuch as the love on the other side is also the desire to be loved. We have a kind of unedifying comedy, in which both unhappy erotic athletes lose the main thing each wants, namely, the other's freedom. Until she loves me she is free, when she loves me her freedom is dissipated, and in neither case can I have it neat. "Hence the lover's perpetual dissatisfaction."[12] In seeking to throw off my freedom by flattening myself into an object for purposes of netting the freedom of the other, my freedom is returned to me when the purpose is fulfilled, but when it is I have lost the freedom of the other as well. One has a sense that Sartre and Simone de Beauvoir, in their remarkable and even monumental love for one another, have sought to escape the metaphysics of erotic disillusionment by pursuing an ideal this analysis ought to render impossible: a mutual fidelity to freedom. Perhaps it is an escape: certainly it is one of the admirable liaisons of modern times. But if it is an escape, it is remarkable, for *Being and Nothingness* leaves no room for escape, either in masochism, in which the lover seeks to become an object *in his own eyes* in a futile

[12] *Ibid.*, pp. 376–77.

endeavor to alienate a freedom which must be presupposed in the very act, or in indifference and hate, or again in sadism—which might be singled out for comment here, since it smokes of Sartrian themes and is the inverse of love, and thus may show love's structure by a kind of indirection.

If love gets its wish, the other becomes an object but, in a way, through the other's own choice, and so the other's choice is an exercise of freedom rather than an enslavement. The sadist then tries to take matters into his own hands and acts upon the other's body in order to incarnate that freedom. When that freedom is coincident with the other's body, in being master over that body I am master over that freedom. Now I have her in bonds or chains. Now I can "do with her what I will." In touching her body I touch *her*. And pain is a marvelous instrument for purposes of incarnation. For pain is an insistent thing: "In pain, facticity invades consciousness."[13] And by applying pain, I aim to embody the other's consciousness by making it nothing but consciousness of her body: what I am after is a collapse of consciousness onto the object, namely the body, which I am perfect master of in the den of torture.

Sartre has in his discussion of sadism a very powerful concept of obscenity, which he contrasts with grace, In the grace of a dancer, for example, the body literally disappears behind its movements, so that even if the dancer in fact is nude, the grace disguises by spiritualizing the flesh. As spectators, we are aware then of movement, and the graced body cannot simultaneously answer to lust: "the nudity of the flesh is wholly present, but it cannot be seen."[14] Obscenity is grace's

[13] *Ibid.*, p. 399.
[14] *Ibid.*, p. 400.

antonym, and consists exactly in the rendering of flesh visible as flesh. It is achieved by putting the occupant of that flesh in a position from which he cannot act with the flesh and is helpless to control its movements, which are subject then to external forces rather than control from within. Jiggling, for instance, is obscene in this sense: "The *obscene* appears when the body adopts postures which . . . reveal the inertia of its flesh."[15] Sartre's analysis of obscenity is a pornographic transform of Bergson's concept of the comic, it having been Bergson's view, roughly, that the basic source of ridiculousness consists in an otherwise autonomous individual becoming subject to mechanical forces acting from without, as classically exemplified in slipping on a banana peel: the sort of thing, Russell archly put it, which "makes M. Bergson laugh." Sadism, then, is the effort to destroy grace, incarnating the other by dispossessing him of freedom over his own body, making his body, hence him, a mere manipulable thing. Of course, *he* must be there to be thus dispossessed: killing him destroys freedom, rather than ensnaring it. And it is after all the freedom of the other which the sadist wants and needs. But where there is a show of freedom on the victim's part, his pleasure is frustrated. In the end, the victim must be brought to humiliate *himself*: *he* must freely identify with his flesh. But then it is *his* choice to do so. Hence failure on the sadist's side.

The question of how long one can endure torture was not an academic question for the captured member of the Resistance during the war. He always had to ask whether he could endure systematic pain in order not to betray his comrades. This issue figures in Sartre's stories as a moral crux, it haunts his play *Morts sans*

---

[15] *Ibid.*, p. 401.

*Sépulture (The Victors)*, it obsessed Malraux, it worried Camus. In the end, however—and Sartre reverts to this in any number of contexts—one chooses the moment at which one yields, when the body is rendered wholly flesh and the heretofore resisting self an incarnated agony: "this distorted and heaving body is the very image of a broken and enslaved freedom."[16] Lack of control over one's body, at least those parts of one's body over which one normally does have control, is indeed deeply humiliating, as in incontinence. The Nazis, Hannah Arendt tells us, ingeniously exploited the excretory functions of prisoners in order to force regressions and crack their wills. And this is the sadist's project as well. But, Sartre argues, the moment of the sadist's success is the moment of his failure. The sadist has to see the body as an instrument to catch the will, but when the end is achieved, the body loses its status as a means and there is nothing to *do* with it any longer—"It is there and it is there for nothing": a disconcerting mass of flesh. Sartre is not especially convincing here. Anything leads to satiation, any tool collapses into a thing when I have no use for it or it loses any use by falling out of the *Zeugganzes* it belonged to. True, he attempts a firm analysis, suggesting that when the victim looks at the sadist, the sadist realizes that his very practice depends upon its acceptance as such by the victim: he is dependent in a kind of hideous symbiosis upon the one over whom he seeks final, total control—like the master by the slave in Hegel. He must therefore turn to something else, sadism ending in a dry defeat. But everything else must end that way too. The motivations of the sadist are, of course, complex, far more so than the torturer who is simply concerned to do his job, pull

---

[16] *Ibid.*, p. 404.

out a bit of information or a confession from the secret knowledge of the victim, and go about his business: *he hasn't failed.* Even so, for all its luridness and incidental truth, Sartre's analysis of sadism only lamely serves its philosophical purposes. And so did the analysis of love.

The claim that conflict is the essence of human relationships must not mislead us. If there is an unremitting war of all against all, it is a special metaphysical sort of war where the stakes are freedom in some special metaphysical sense, which has nothing much to do with political freedom or economic enslavement. And it leaves room for all sorts of cooperative enterprises— like working together with pals to bring out *Les Temps Modernes*, to choose a Parisian instance. Sartre would have been as aware of this as anyone, and it cannot have been his intention to deny plain facts. The outcome of all those futile projects catalogued under Concrete Relations with Others merely underscores the metaphysically inalienable freedom of others and ourselves. One cannot but treat men as ends and not as means the moment one is aware of one's own freedom and collaterally of the freedom of the other: by the very advent of self-consciousness one realizes the Categorical Imperative, and it is presupposed in all these attempts to violate it. So all of these relations are exercises in bad faith in the sense that one condition of morality as construed by Kant is implicit. They are, indeed, moral postures all, inasmuch as they are assumed in the full recognition that the other is an agent and a free being. Sartre's personages are not tyrants who see men *merely* as means. (The tyrant in this sense is not even indifferent—so far as indifference is a moral attitude in which one must know the facts in order to disregard them—he is just blandly unaware of other men as *men*; *his* world is *the* world, because he has not attained to a consciousness of other consciousnesses.) If they did not first recognize other freedoms, there could not be conflicts of the sort their enterprises exemplify. The existence of other consciousnesses penetrates the structure of their own, and if they did not acknowledge those freedoms, they would have nothing to try to capture.

Meanwhile, we might note that conflict remains the original relationship to one another in the *Critique de la raison dialectique*—a work devoted less to ontology than to the social psychological possibilities of group life. Here the focus and occasions of conflict are material and economic, rather than consequences of moral pathology, as in *Being and Nothingness*; they are due to material scarcity and metabolic requirements, rather than to the spiritual ambition to reclaim the world for oneself, a matter of eating rather than moral domination. "Our history . . . emerged and developed in the permanent context of a field of tension engendered by scarcity."[17] And this defines the relationship in which we stand to one another, as competing consumers: to recognize oneself as having material requirements simultaneously discloses the other as "the simple possibility of consuming an object one needs." Each, in short, discovers in each "the material possibility of his own annihilation through the annihilation of a material object of primary necessity."[18] This does not, of course, entail that men are inherently oppressors—the view remains in the *Critique* that man has no permanent nature, so that men could be humane as well as swine—"and yet, as

[17] R. D. Cumming, *The Philosophy of Jean-Paul Sartre*, p. 436. As the *Critique de la raison dialectique* has not been completely translated, I refer to the translations in Cumming's anthology, except for the item in note 23, which he has not included.
[18] *Ibid.*

## Shame: or, the Problem of Other Minds | 133

long as the sway of scarcity is not yet ended, there will be in each man and in everyone an inert structure of inhumanity which is, in short, nothing but the material negation insofar as it is interiorized."[19] This internalized structure of inhumanity is externalized as violence, perceived always as counter-violence in the respect that I am violent toward those whom I am required by the structure of my praxis to believe violently disposed toward me, as we compete for the same scarce goods. Violence as counter-violence is a reflection in a dark mirror of love as the desire to be loved. But since anyone can compete with me and I with anyone, the object of violence is men, not just this or that particular man: "It is man *qua* man . . . whom I am attacking; it is man, and nothing else, that I hate in the enemy, that is myself as Other, and it is certainly I whom I wish to destroy in him in order to prevent him from destroying me, actually, in my body."[20] As with the fields of sophisticated tension in *Being and Nothingness*, which simultaneously unite and divide us as hostile freedoms, scarcity here, at this more primitive material level, unites and divides us: "We are united by the fact that we all inhabit a world defined by scarcity."[21] I, others, and the material world are melded together in a field of praxis by our several needs, by the niggardliness of nature in furnishing enough for our satisfaction, and so the structural competition in which this thrusts us with one another is inevitable. But since scarcity is contingent, this analysis permits a more hopeful attitude, at least in principle—unless the conflicts painted in *Being and Nothingness* await us when we enter the

---

[19] *Ibid.*, p. 438.
[20] *Ibid.*, p. 442.
[21] *Ibid.*, p. 445.

material paradise of each according to his needs, others being hell even in the classless society.

*Being and Nothingness* denies the possibility of a structure of a *we*, my consciousness always being *mine* —even if, perhaps necessarily if, penetrated by awareness of others. True, I can experience a *feeling* of "we," but this alone cannot "constitute an ontological structure of human-reality," since it is psychological rather than ontological. The "we" is always experienced, as anything else must be, by an individual consciousness, and it is not required that those with whom I feel it should feel it in their turn, and even if they do so, even if we all feel as one and as part of a community, the feeling is distributed through our several consciousnesses and so is just a sum of individual feelings, rather than "an inter-subjective consciousness [or] a new being which surpasses and encircles its parts as a synthetic whole."[22] So "being-with"—what Heidegger spoke of as *mitsein*—is only a specialization of the structure of being-for-others. It is so whether we approach the matter from the perspective of subject or object, for Sartre recognizes a possibility that my relationship with another may acquire a certain status as an object upon the appearance of a Third who perceives us as part of the same structure, as fighters, say, or lovers: the Third sees *two* people fighting or fucking *one another*, constituting them as an "us." But this presupposes, Sartre says, still an individual consciousness, namely that of the Third, with whom a conflict of much the same sort as we have been discussing arises, partly based on the insistence that *us* is not a single entity but two individuals in the end sundered from one another and from the Third. So there is in Sartre a skepticism re-

[22] *Being and Nothingness*, p. 414.

## Shame: or, the Problem of Other Minds | 135

garding the possible primacy of any kind of group life, any life that resists collapse into a constellation of individual consciousnesses in which it exists as an object —though why the consciousness of sociality does not become the sociality of consciousness never gets worked out. In any case, this becomes a matter of considerable concern to Sartre in the *Critique*, which discusses among other things the morphology of groups.

The typical group is the serial one, whose example is that of a sundry collection of persons waiting for a bus. The bus is a common object which may be said to unite them as a group, but then they perceive one another only as competitors for seats and otherwise are in a relationship of characterless indifference. Most social groups are of this order, but Sartre does speak at a certain point of *groups-in-fusion*, and supposes the mob at the storming of the Bastille might have been one. The case is exceedingly complex as analyzed. The individuals are, through a common threat, fused into a common freedom. "It is not that I am myself in the other, it is that within this praxis there is no other, there are only myself [*il y a des moi-même*]."[23] It is impossible to deny that it posits itself for itself . . . or, if you prefer, a new structure must be taken into account—the *group consciousness*."[24] This is quite another matter, obviously, from the "we-consciousness" of *Being and Nothingness*, as though the group here were the *pour-soi* writ large, existing, Sartre thinks, for itself as a group. His analysis of how the individual consciousnesses can be overcome by a group consciousness in which they nevertheless participate is exceedingly intricate, but under any circumstances the new entity is ephemeral, degenerating

---

[23] *Critique de la raison dialectique*, p. 420.
[24] Cumming, *op. cit.*, p. 423.

rapidly, and the attempt to will it into existence, or legislate it, say by the members of the group declaring through some form of oath that the group exists as a group, is futile: "the group has not and cannot have the ontological status that it claims in its praxis."[25]

There may be such sublime moments of togetherness, in which our apartnesses appear obliterated and transcended. Georges Sorel imagined they might be achieved through a general strike given the status of a myth. But, to paraphrase Sartre, we are dealing with something sociological rather than ontological here, and the possibility along with its rareness merely heightens a deep pessimism concerning the possibility of a genuinely moral, not to say altruistic mode of conduct toward one another. If our radical selfishness can be overcome only in moments of moral sublimity, there is very little hope indeed. But in compensation it may be said that the actual structures of ethics can hardly depend upon such unpredictable and essentially transitory phrases of transindividuality. Morality, as Aristotle said, is made for men, and so must have application in the most ordinary circumstances of human intercourse: to base an ethics on them would be like basing our concept of cognition on experiences which happen rarely if at all. But I defer treatment of the possibility or morality until my final chapter.

I should like now to take up a point touched upon *en passant* in connection with abjuration under torture, for that issue connects with an extraordinary feature of Sartre's philosophy which integrates a great deal of what he has said about freedom and the responsibility one has for one's life, one's choices, and one's world.

[25] *Ibid.*, p. 445.

The moment of surrender, of yielding to one's body, of becoming one with the suffering it is being made to undergo, can always be postponed. I might always have held out another second, and then another. So the question of why I yielded when I did, or at all, cannot be shirked. Each of my actions could have been otherwise or forborne, and this must follow from my utter freedom. But in one respect it is correct to say that though in a deep sense I *could* have held out, I *would* not have done so. I would not because of the sort of person I am. And the sort of person I am, whether one who endures torture until death or one who confesses at the mere threat of it, thinking my skin more worth saving than that of my fellows, is altogether a matter of my having chosen to be it. This Sartre speaks of as my original choice, which is the notion I want now to describe.

Analytical philosophers concerned with the topic of human action have laid down a distinction between the causes and the reasons for an action. At times they have stated the concept of action in these terms: a piece of behavior is not an action if it is caused; it is one only if performed for a reason, or only if it is at least relevant to ask what the person's reason was for his performance. Naturally, something can be done "for no reason," but if this is true in a given case, the person who denies that there was a reason at least accepts the legitimacy of the question. For merely mechanical behavior, say the breakdown of protein molecules, the question has no application: there is no reason because there could have been none, since the behavior in question was not "done." In such cases, the question of why, for what reason, is conceptually ruled out. There can then be only causes. Reasons, again, can be regarded as a species of cause, and an action thought of as a performance which, if caused at all, is caused by a reason, but the connection between a reason and an action involves more than is thought to be required by ordinary causes in relation to their effects: for one thing, the reason is formulated in terms of the action it explains, where it is a mark of ordinary causes that they may be formulated without reference to their effects. This was why Hume was able to argue that causes and effects are logically independent of one another, whereas modern philosophers have been tempted to say, with some justification, though it must be carefully stated, that reasons and actions are not in this sense logically independent.

Sartre exploits something like this distinction intuitively in his discussion of freedom and action, and his argument is more or less as follows: a reason specifies what it is in the world that I mean to change by means of my action. But that objective state of affairs does not and cannot all by itself cause the action; it does so only if constituted a reason by the agent. The agent, as it were, transforms these states of affairs into causes by regarding them as reasons for action. Briefly, I determine which circumstances and events are going to explain my actions. Thus I may close the window because the noise outside is intolerable. But its being intolerable explains the action only because I found it so. And this is generally the case. The very having of reasons implies a stand outside the causal order, and involves a "double nihilation," as Sartre says: the agent posits an ideal state of affairs which the world at this point is *not* and which itself is *not* a present reality. But the critical point is that "no factual state . . . is capable by itself of motivating any act whatsoever . . . [and] no factual state can determine consciousness to apprehend it as a *negatité* or as a lack."[26] So if, in the

[26] *Being and Nothingness*, pp. 435–36.

## Shame: or, the Problem of Other Minds | 139

end, my actions have causes, these are such only through having been constituted causes by my mode of apprehending them, and all explanations of human action have to be filtered through the agent's way of reading the world, and not with reference to the world alone. In fact this may be supported by considering that a man may wholly misperceive the world, so that there is no objective state of affairs to explain his action. He may recoil before what he takes to be a snake but is only a serpentine stick. Still, his reason was "to avoid getting bit," and his situation was determined by his perception of it.

So, there may be no action without a cause.[27] But this, instead of supporting a universal determinism, is precisely what is required by the fact of freedom: I *make* the world such that my actions can be explained through my apprehension of it. "There is freedom only in situation, and there is a situation only through freedom." Consciousness lays down the conditions of its bearer's conduct.

Sartre calls this the Paradox of Freedom, but there is, if my account is correct, nothing paradoxical in it at all. The thesis combines the Principle of Sufficient Reason with the constitutive character of consciousness: each of us is free only to the extent that we determine what are to be causes of our acts. The constitution of causes is what makes choosing sensible and even logically unavoidable, but of course I have no choice as to whether, only how, to choose: I am, as Sartre characteristically puts it, condemned to be free. I am so because there is no consciousness without a world of which it is conscious, but then the way the world reveals itself to me has to be referred back to the structures

[27] *Ibid.*, p. 489.

of my consciousness. Or, to use another of his phrases, *I* am never the foundation of my freedom. If actions are explained with reference to the structures of freedom, freedom itself cannot be explained that way. It is the brute, primitive, given fact of my existence. I cannot choose not to choose, except within the framework of choices, where not-choosing is a kind of choice, as when I choose no one for my wife. The moment I exist I am already, and cannot escape having to be, a maker of choices. To be the foundation of my freedom would mean being able to choose to be free. And this makes no sense.

Sartre's analysis of motivation, whatever may be the consequences he draws from it, seems to me largely impeccable. We may not wish to endorse his vocabulary, e.g., that "contingency and facticity are really one." Or again, "Human-reality everywhere encounters resistance and obstacles which it has not created, but these resistances and obstacles have meaning only in and through the free choice which human-reality *is*."[28] But the thought behind these formulations is clear and, I believe, philosophically defensible. In terms of what he says, it follows that my place in society, my biology, and my past are not sheer determinants of my conduct, but attain an explanatory role only with reference to the interpretation I give of them. It is only verbally paradoxical of Sartre to say that we choose to be born and that we choose to die: what he means is that we choose what meaning our births and deaths happen to have for us. So it is a fair conclusion that "I am responsible for everything, in fact, except for my very responsibility, for I am not the foundation of my be-

[28] *Ibid.*, pp. 486, 489.

## Shame: or, the Problem of Other Minds | 141

ing."[29] I am, that is, responsible for all the interpreted facts. But for consciousness there are no other facts.

It must follow that no causes of actions lie outside consciousness, are *unconscious* causes. For this reason a wholly different sort of psychoanalysis is required than the sort we have learned about from Freud and his followers, who may disagree with their master in various ways and yet share with him the theory that there are hidden causes of human behavior. Sartre proposes in its place what he calls existentialist psychoanalysis, which has choice as its core, and is one of his most fascinating innovations.

Given that something is a cause of my action only if I constitute it as such, is there no further explanation of why I constitute *it* as a cause and in just the way I do constitute it? Could I not have constituted other things as causes of my actions, structured the world differently, live quite different possibilities out? To be sure, we have invoked the idea that freedom is freedom, and has no "foundation." Still, one's schedule of choices is not chaotic and utterly unpredictable. We know about one another and often a man knows about himself the sorts of choices he will make, that *given* a choice he will go one way rather than another. How are we to account for this? It has always been an obsession of Sartre's to have an answer to this sort of question. A favorite case of his has been Flaubert: "Why," he asks, "does Flaubert turn to writing rather than to painting or music for . . . symbolic satisfaction?"[30] The question is posed over and over again in Sartre's writings, and it gets a massive concrete answer in his last study of

[29] *Ibid.*, p. 555.
[30] *Ibid.*, p. 559.

Flaubert, whose life, he feels, like every life, is a permeating order. "This book," he writes in the preface to *L'Idiot de la famille*, "seeks to prove that . . . each bit of information put in its place becomes the portion of a whole which does not cease to work itself out and, at the same time, reveals a deep homogeneity with every other one."[31] But our concern is less with specific answers to such specific questions than with the philosophical principle that underlies the legitimacy of all such questions. Sartre's objection, as we have seen before, to Freud and to Marx, is that they fail in principle to enable us to understand why just *this* man or woman responded in just *this* way to the supposedly common Oedipal situation or class condition, the individual being swamped by the general theory. Unless a theory of human beings allows for this utter degree of individualization, it is incomplete or even inconsistent with the basic structures of its basic subjects—individual persons. We need, then, specific answers to specific questions, and a kind of "veritable irreducible." But more than just a very detailed description is needed: we want to understand why he is who he is and his world what *it* is; the form of answer to this, and that which gives a unity to someone's entire life, is what Sartre speaks of as the *ultimate project* of the individual in question.

The concept of the ultimate project has a complex metaphysical task to perform, which goes far beyond the theoretical enfranchisement of the sorts of biographies Sartre has devoted himself to in one dimension of his literary life: it plays something like the role the soul plays in traditional schemes, accounting for the unity of a person from stage to stage of his life. Sartre, of course, would repudiate the notion of a soul as an

[31] *L'Idiot de la famille*, p. 1.

## Shame: or, the Problem of Other Minds | 143

underlying and inalterable substrate on which biographical events are hung like laundry on a line. But still, a person is a totality, the bits of his life belong together, penetrating one another the way we saw the qualities of a thing to do, and the original project is the principle of this unity, as the *thing* is the principle of the series of it interbleeding appearances, in each of which it is wholly manifest. He is not just a series of discrete episodes, as Hume came close to believing: "in each inclination, in each tendency the person expresses himself completely."[32] So each act and gesture holds, if we can read it, the key to all the others. But this, even if true, represents the position of the outsider to a life, that of the biographer or historian, and the question we must consider has instead to do with the *lived* unity which is externally presented as a totality. In invoking the notion of an original project here, we are invoking something which, however different in many ways, is after all not so remarkably different from a soul.

Let us work this out, using one of Sartre's best examples. A man is out hiking with friends. At a certain point, he throws himself on the ground from exhaustion: he can walk no farther. None of his comrades do this, though they have about the same physical shape and muscular endowment as he, and they have hiked just as far. Why should he have chosen just now to find his fatigue unbearable? They have chosen it as something to be borne and want to press ahead to the camp. These diverging choices, Sartre argues, have to be explained "within the perspective of a larger choice in which [they] would be integrated as a secondary structure." Their choice, like that of their comrade on the ground, is emblematic of the way they have chosen

---

[32] *Being and Nothingness*, p. 563.

to live their lives. A man who abandons himself to fatigue is going to be a self-indulgent person, treating himself "to a thousand little passing gluttonies, to a thousand little desires, a thousand little weaknesses."[33] The point is perfectly general: there are no isolated symptoms, even in psychoanalysis, only signs of a "free and global project" which the analyst has to bring to the surface, as it were, before he can tell what anything means. "I choose myself as a whole in a world which is a whole."[34]

In *Morts sans sépulture*, a group of captured *maquisards* are questioned one by one, and each ponders whether he will be able to endure the torture he knows awaits him. In the end, not talking becomes more important than keeping their secret, winning out against their captors more important than not betraying their comrades. One of them wonders how he will hold up, feeling he does not know *himself* as a self until he sees how he comes through this extreme trial. He cries out, he would tell anything he knew: "And now I know myself," he says. His friends remonstrate with him. "We are not made to live always at the limits of ourselves," one of them says, wisely enough. Most of us would agree. Most of us would say that what we know is just that we would break under torture: and why should this be the *real* us? But if Sartre is right, this is too reassuring. The episode is never so extreme that we could not have known it would happen as it did happen, that it is one with the whole of life as we have lived it. To be sure, some men are lucky and die in their beds— "Cowards like me without ever knowing they are." Extremity reveals a pattern that was always there to be

---

[33] *Ibid.*, pp. 455, 456.
[34] *Ibid.*, p. 461.

## Shame: or, the Problem of Other Minds | 145

seen, probably even in the way and order in which a man tied his shoes.

Our basic freedom, then, lies less in our power to choose than to *choose* to choose, in the respect that the primal and original choice determines a *style* of choosing, and the style is the man himself, as Buffon said. Choosing to choose does *not* mean that each act of will requires a separate act of will to get it moving; for that would lead to an infinite regression. But still, there is no freedom, Sartre feels, unless we are free in this higher-order mode, choosing in such a way as to define our lives. This concept, needless to say, raises a large class of difficult questions. The past, for example, was exactly to have no constraint upon the present—unless I choose my past, making (consistent with the analysis just worked out) certain episodes of my past causally relevant to my present and future. So how can an original choice as a datable historical episode continue to determine my choices *now*? And does "original" mean "earlier in time" or merely "more basic than" some present choice? Sartre seems to have supposed the first as well as the second, seeking out that *moment* in the life of Baudelaire or Genet or Flaubert when the die was cast, the mold formed for everything that followed. That is what existential analysis comes to. But there may be another answer, though I offer it diffidently. It is that in each choice I do more than choose a specific course of action; rather, I choose a style of choosing. So the original choice is made in every choice. For choosings, let us remember, are not serially ordered isolated episodes. With each choice I am integrating all previous choices into a totality. I am, then, not just choosing to take the bus instead of walking: I am choosing the sort of man I am and the sort of life I have and the sort of world I live in. My responsibilities are *enormous*. As much so as God's. If every choice is an original choice, there are no gratuitous or meaningless acts. And since at each instant I am choosing a world, the world that is mine is up to me.

This view requires immense philosophical elaboration, which it goes beyond the limits of this book to pursue. But it plainly has an implication for moral conduct: namely, that we are not to evaluate an action in its own right and alone but only as an ingredient in a tapestry of choices that total up to an entire life—as though there were an implicit, almost categorical imperative binding upon us at every moment, to so choose that the form of life the choice implies is one we would be willing to live always. The question always before us is what sort of person we are making of ourselves. This brings us to the threshold of Sartre's theory of values.

Anguish: or, Factual Beliefs and Moral Attitudes

# V

*Being and Nothingness* concludes by raising a set of questions regarding values and their relationship to our freedom, and promises to answer them on the plane of ethical theory in a further study. That study has not as yet been published, and perhaps Sartre has not as yet written it, it being one of a number of promised, unachieved works—like the fourth volume of his probably abandoned novel *Roads to Liberty*, the second volume of the *Critique de la raison dialectique*, and a study of Tintoretto, a sketch of which appeared in one of the volumes of essays Sartre calls *Situations*. Though an interesting if stolid essay by Simone de Beauvoir, *The Ethics of Ambiguity*, attempts to work out the implications of an existentialist ethic, and it is difficult to suppose that Sartre did not discuss every word of it with his consort, anything one says on the subject of value in Sartre's philosophy must remain speculative and structural, even if certain possibilities appear to be ruled out by everything written by him so far. Perhaps one can locate Sartre's position by thinking for a moment of the schedule of meta-ethical positions which has tended until quite recent times to dominate moral philosophy in the Anglo-Saxon world, and I shall accordingly begin with that.

Briefly, the basic question, to which these positions are responses, is whether moral propositions can be straightforwardly assessed in terms of truth and falsity, whether, for instance, "$x$ is (morally) good" or "$y$ is (ethically) right" are propositions about the world in the way in which we may suppose "$x$ is red" or "$y$ is running" to be. If they are, then there is something one might call moral knowledge, and the possibility then exists that the world itself has moral qualities on footing with other qualities like colors, or at least that moral terms can be defined exhaustively by sets of incontestably descriptive terms, so that the propositions which use these terms are, by dint of such translation, finally about and only about the way the world is. The remaining position holds that these propositions are not at all descriptive, that their function, whatever it may be, is not or not exclusively to state facts or to describe things and events—to express moral *truths*—but rather to express attitudes and feelings, or to commend the things they are about, or to persuade others to take certain positive or negative attitudes toward those things, and the like. Here positions vary, but a core of agreement is to the effect that there is ultimately nothing cognitive about moral propositions, that at best we can tell from the fact that a person uses them what he believes, but never anything further about whether what he believes is true, for truth and falsity have no application here at all. Accordingly, those who subscribe to this position are negatively characterized as noncognitivists in ethical theory.

Though Sartre's approach has never been primarily linguistic, the view we must identify him with is a qualified noncognitivism. At least there are no moral facts, no values which objectively attach to things *en-soi*, and it was precisely the ontological mistake of the Serious Man to believe that there were. But at the same time it is fairly plain that values do appear in the world as it is *lived*, and that they are inseparable from the meanings which hold one's world together through the situational structures of the *pour-soi*. So with reference to *my* world (for any "me"), evaluative propositions are as descriptive as any used to characterize the situations one lives in. They must, as we saw, be invoked in the internal explanations of human action, since all of these arise in response to certain perceived *lacks* in the world. So values, as lacks, have as much an objective foothold in things as the *négatités*. Nothingness, too, let us recall, was excluded in principle from the *en-soi*. Belonging thus to the same category as nothingness, values are woven into the fabric of the world-for-us. And indeed it would not be possible to engage with a world without values of at least this degree of objectivity, since values are generated by the very structure of engagement. "Reflective consciousness," Sartre writes, "can be properly called a moral consciousness since it cannot arise without at the same moment disclosing values."[1] Inasmuch as (and to its detriment), the concept of the world-for-us—which is perhaps the positive contribution of phenomenology and Continental philosophy generally—has never been

---

[1] *Being and Nothingness*, p. 95.

particularly marked in meta-ethical disputations within the analytical movement, Sartre's position introduces a benign complication. He is a noncognitivist so far as the world *en-soi* is concerned and a cognitivist with regard to the world *pour-nous*, and this, because we are after all in both worlds at once, is the gist of the ambiguity of which Simone de Beauvoir makes such heavy weather.

"Human reality is that by which values arrive in the world," Sartre says,[2] just as it is that by which nothingness does, which means that we do not find values there ready and waiting when we enter the world, but they are generated as a condition of our entry. Wittgenstein writes at *Tractatus* 6.41, "In the world, everything is as it is and happens as it does happen. *In it* there is no value—and if there were, it would be of no value." I believe what he means is that values are not further items for a disinterested intellect to take note of in surveying the contents of the world as given, and if by chance there should be values in this sense—solid as apples, there like dogs—they would not answer to the sorts of demands which *having* value presupposes. And we must understand this to mean that things have value —this would be so even if there were values which also were things—only in terms of an action relationship and with reference to a notion of meaning which has no place in the final objective description of the world. "The sense of the world," Wittgenstein elaborates, "must lie outside the world." So whether or not values have value in this sense, would be a question like whether or not apples or dogs do; and since all the important and essential questions about values lie here, it would be an interesting but largely irrelevant fact about the world that it should house such creatures as values.

[2] *Ibid.*, p. 93.

## Anguish | 151

And this is Sartre's view as well: when values are realized, they are no longer of value. So through the very nature of the concept "having value" descriptivism must be wrong, all the issues having to do not with the world but with our relationship with it. Values escape our ontology and derive their substance through the way in which they escape it.

Early in *Being and Nothingness*, Sartre states that values are "demands which lay claim to a foundation." The emphasis must be placed on the term "demands"; Sartre goes on to say that the foundation in question cannot be being itself, "for every value which would have its ideal nature in being would thereby cease even to be a value."[3] This sounds utterly like Wittgenstein. And again, in what would sound like a paraphrase were there the possibility that Sartre had known Wittgenstein's text, "it does not deliver itself to a contemplative intuition which would apprehend it as *being* value." No: its being lies in its exigency, in the demand it makes to be realized, so values are "revealed only to an active freedom which makes it exist as value by the sole fact of recognizing it as such." It follows (Sartre believes) that "my freedom is the unique foundation of values, and nothing, absolutely nothing, justifies me in adopting this or that particular value, or particular scale of values." Still, it is part of the formulation that values demand a *foundation*, and I am not altogether certain how this is to be interpreted. Kant proposed that we should so act that the principle, or maxim, of our action could consistently be willed as a universal law of nature, and there is in this thought a clue to what Sartre means. To accept the demand in which a value consists is to believe that the value could be realized in being, though

[3] *Ibid.*, p. 38.

—and this is true of Kant's theory as well—as soon as it is realized this way, as soon as the value coalesces into a *fact*, it is no longer a value. For being now just part of the way the world is, a demand that it be realized would be inoperative, and the value is bound up with the demand. So in a way the demands cannot be met, because in becoming a thing, the value stops being a value.

There is a sort of paradox here, if one wishes to perceive it that way, in that ideals cannot be realized and still be ideals. If the maxim which we will were indeed a fact of nature, the exercise of the will would have no place, it having been Sartre's teaching that the *en-soi* by definition is independent of the will. This may in the end be a triviality, just as a doubt once removed is no longer a doubt, or a question answered is no longer felt as a question by someone who knows the answer. But it ensures at least that values cannot be matters of knowledge, if knowledge must always be of what is the case: for, to repeat one last time, if values were what is the case, they would have no value. So values are inherently pragmatic matters.

This general line of argument has, I believe, a certain interest and plausibility. To believe that something is good or right is almost to be incapable of believing that there is no more to the matter than this, that something is good in just the way in which it is red. Rather, it is to believe that the belief in question has an altogether different sort of grounding than simply correspondence to the world. But, at the same time, to believe that something is good is *not* to believe that all there is to goodness is believing that something has it. More than merely having an attitude is required in ethics. How could men argue or fight for what they believe to be good if all

## Anguish | 153

they believed was that goodness consisted in moral beliefs and attitudes? What, after all, is more serious for life than the pursuit of values? So something in excess of what noncognitivism allows is required by the very having of moral beliefs, even if this excess is not mere correspondence with some supposed moral fact. This is why values seem to demand some foundation. But the burden of Sartre's analysis is that there is no foundation save one's freedom, that value is a matter of choosing, and that nothing ultimately justifies choosing one way rather than another.

The recognition of these truths Sartre speaks of as anguish. As before, we may not *feel* anguish, and, even if we do, this is not relevant to the concept. Anguish is only the recognition that our values are our own, and due ultimately to us, and that nothing and no one, not God or the Church or the Party, can in any serious way support our choice. If any of them do, it is because we have chosen them as support, so that the foundations of moral choice are internal to choosing and cannot justify it from without. Sartre, if anyone, must be master of the concept of anguish in this sense. But if he *feels* any anguish in making his moral pronouncements, it is marvelously hidden. He condemns and approves with the confidence of a pope. I suppose he feels infallible in a way, but only because the notion of fallibility has no application, and his opponents might recognize, were they to accept his theory, that they are no *less* authoritative than he. Truth or falsity have no possible bearing. Since values have no connection with understanding the world, they can only concern changing it. It happens that the changes Sartre has endorsed are intuitively humane, and that his heart is as a matter of spontaneity in the right place. But his schedule of values has no more an objective grounding, if he is right, than the values of his enemies: oppressors and dictators and torturers and exploiters.

Sartre naturally puts his own light on these matters. Since it is through me that values exist, since I am the foundation of my values, as, and for the same reason as, I am the foundation of my world, I *myself* can have no foundation whatever. For my being is not grounded in the being of any other thing or person, this being part of the meaning of freedom. Sartre spends a considerable time in discussing freedom's logically futile endeavor to put a ground under itself—futile because if it succeeded it would be freedom no longer, just as values grounded in being would be values no longer. Or we can put this in the terms of "lack" which Sartre and naturally Simone de Beauvoir favor. Things themselves have no lacks; "they are what they are," the holes in things being part of what they are, not something they need to have filled. Only relative to a use or need do we speak of them as lacking. So lacks, like *négatités*, generally are laid down by the engaged consciousness (and there are no disengaged ones). But consciousness itself lacks something and will always lack it. What it lacks is being. "In its coming into existence human reality grasps itself as an incomplete being." Moreover, "human reality is a perpetual surpassing toward a coincidence with itself which is never given." And were it to be given, the *pour-soi* would lose its character and its world, what gives the world and itself meaning always being outside either. So "it could not attain the in-itself without losing itself as for-itself."[4] The pursuit of being is the constant and ultimate futility. And this is what I meant by saying that the value of values is

[4] *Ibid.*, pp. 89-90.

## Anguish | 155

connected with the fact that they escape us, not because they cannot be realized but because when realized they are not values. At the very end of his discussion, Sartre asks whether freedom itself might take itself as a value, and what would happen to the concept of value if it did so? He concludes with the question and gives no answer. I am uncertain whether an answer could be given or what it would look like, since the value in question could not be realized in principle, freedom being precisely that which lacks being: and what kind of demand does the concept of demanding itself make?

In any case, there can be no question of generating an ethic on the basis of Sartre's book, for although one might want to say that we should always act so as to maximize and never minimize our freedom and the freedom of others, and take this as a sort of final imperative, the freedom in question would have to be political and would have nothing to do with the *metaphysical* freedom which the book defines. *That* freedom is total and absolute, in and out of jail, as much so for the father of a family as for the irresponsible night hawk of Saint-Germain-des-Prés. As Descartes says, our liberty is equal to that of God, our freedom is perfect, it being only our understanding which is limited, and our knowledge. So it would be an imperative on which we could not relevantly act. And with this, I believe, Sartre implicitly concurs. "Ontology itself cannot formulate ethical precepts," he says at the end,[5] and echoes in support of this claim a famous point of Hume's according to whom we cannot deduce how we ought to act from any description, however exhaustive, of the way the world is. "Ontology," Sartre says, "is concerned solely with what is, and we cannot possibly derive imperatives

[5] *Ibid.*, p. 625.

from ontology's indicatives." So any ethic will be consistent with what we are, except such ethics as may have ontological presuppositions at variance with the discoveries of *Being and Nothingness*, such as those of the Serious Man. But even his value scheme would work, the fault lying only in his meta-ethical beliefs, though an interesting technical question remains as to whether meta-ethics is itself ethically neutral, and I suppose it would be in terms of coping with that question that one would have to determine finally if there could be an existentialist ethics, a specific *morale* of ambiguity. All Sartre tells us is that from the viewpoint of ontology, "all human activities are equivalent."[6] "It comes to the same thing whether one gets drunk alone or is a leader of nations." (He insinuates that the drunk may in fact come off better, Sartre's taste for shocking his readers being insistable.) So, finally, there is nothing external to ourselves to which we can legitimately appeal to decide how, at the moral level, we ought to choose, or what.

The discussion thus far has concerned what one might term the ultimate justification of one's value scheme. From the point of view of ontology, nothing of the sort is available, and in this respect only, one simply chooses. But once engaged, once having made one's original choice, justifications are always in principle available from within the scheme itself, so it is important that we distinguish between what we might call external questions of justification and internal ones. The point, of course, is that in choosing a form or style of life, one also chooses the sorts of consideration one is henceforward to be guided by in framing one's patterns of justification. Hence, internally to a system of choices one

[6] *Ibid.*, p. 627.

Anguish | 157

often, even typically, may justify taking one course of action rather than another, this following from the concept of actions and reasons outlined above. All Sartre so far has said is that we cannot justify choosing between systems, that decisions of principle, as they have been termed by the British moral philosopher R. H. Hare, are indifferent to all such questions. But even so, internal and external factors at times collide, dilemmas arise that can only be resolved by a decision leaving one with a moral price to pay whichever way one goes, and Sartre's sensitivity to such conflicts is one of his major contributions to moral theory. I should like to conclude by describing this aspect of his thought.

No account of Sartre's philosophy would be complete if it did not mention a now famous question he reports as having been put to him by a young man during World War II. The young man was faced with the dilemma of whether to join the Resistance and leave his aged and dependent mother, or to stay with her and implicitly to acquiesce in the political obscenity of the German occupation. Either choice left him with intolerable consequences. And he came to Sartre seeking a way out. Sartre gave the only answer his system allowed him to give. "Who could help him choose?" he wrote later. "Certainly not Christian doctrine, since both choices satisfy the criteria of a Christian choice. Nor again Kantian ethics, for he cannot consistently treat everyone as an end, for someone will have to be treated as means. I had only one answer to give. 'You're free, choose. . . .' No general ethic can show you what is to be done."[7] It is not merely, here, that nothing will finally count as a sign or as evidence that one has made the right choice—in part because in accepting a

[7] *Existentialism*, pp. 36, 38.

sign or evidence one has already made one's decision, one has already decided by what one's choice is to be determined; and in part because the issue is an external one, between two schemes that cannot simultaneously be lived. In effect, it is a choice between lives. One cannot live two sorts of lives at once. But within a life the question can arise in an agonizing way which sort of life is going to be lived from now on, and a price has to be paid either way: the new life is going to be contaminated by values carried over from the old one. So the decision is never altogether clean.

We are not told how the young man finally decided, but however the moral drama was worked out, it had a deep decision at its core and cannot have had a happy ending, though we can imagine factual changes which might have eased the pressure: the war might have ended, or the mother died, or a long-lost brother returned to take over the filial responsibilities. But these would be so many *deis ex machina*, and do not affect the dramatic structures of the situation, which have, I believe, important and neglected philosophical features. Life is not only a burden of unremitting choice which *I* cannot throw off except by yet another choice. It at times thrusts us, and at any time can thrust us, into situations of extremity, which Sartre's student but illustrates, where choice is forced and cannot be rationally resolved. Conflicting demands put us under equal but counterposed obligations, so that in fulfilling one we in the nature of the case violate the other, and there is no neutral standpoint which it lies within our power to occupy. There is a kind of optimism in moral philosophy, according to which all such conflicts only are *prima facie*, and given any pair of seemingly incompatible demands one is always, under deep considerations and in the long moral run, preferable to the other: just one of them always has to be the greater good or the lesser evil. So there are no *deep* moral conflicts—though moral *knowledge*, if we may speak this way, may at any given time be inadequate for purposes of determining which is the preferred course of action. It is, then, a kind of *a priori* of moral philosophy that there is a morally right decision, if we but knew how to find out what it was. There will always perhaps be a price to pay. But in terms of this *a priori*, the price we pay will be lower than the one we would have had to pay had we chosen the other way instead. This optimism is, I think, subscribed to by utilitarianism—what other moral philosophy speaks so readily of moral knowledge, and which other regards the only moral tragedies to be due finally to deficiencies in moral knowledge? But it is not obvious that utilitarianism is right; and if Sartre's account is right, utilitarianism is wrong. There may just be, on the deepest level, blankly irreconcilable and equally urgent demands with only the possibility of a hopeless choice and no way out.

Sartre has always, especially in his dramatic works, been sensitive to such conflicts. One may take a course of action that will undoubtedly promote human welfare—but only at a cost it is impossible for one who has internalized what *human* welfare means not to be appalled by. In *Dirty Hands*, the character of Hugo, an intellectual and an assassin, has only the most abstract conception of human welfare and is prepared to sacrifice, since such sacrifice means little to him to begin with, all manner of human factors in the name of the revolution. His patron and victim, Hoederer, is immeasurably more mature; there is no question who is the finer person. "As for me," Hoederer says, "I have dirty hands. Up to the elbows! I have plunged them into shit and into blood. And then? Do you think one can govern innocently?"[8] And Hugo says, to be sure *péniblement*, "One does not make a revolution with flowers." What is admirable about Hoederer is that he *knows* he is paying a price, and what is shallow and even hateful about Hugo is that there is not even a price. Needless to say, Hugo is guided by an abstract ideal of humanity in view of which *men as they are* have no interest for him, and to which they may be sacrificed with impunity. "And I," Hoederer says, "I love them as they are. With all their *saloperies* and their vices. . . . For me, a man more or less in the world counts." So Hoederer has had to do evil, and knows that he has and that it was evil. He lives in the knowledge that there is no rational exculpation at a higher level. This, I believe, is what the concept of anguish must finally mean: a recognition of freedom as hateful, in a situation where there is recourse only to it.

The logician Bas Van Frassen writes this way:

> The reasonable man will strike a balance between the moral duty and moral ideals. Perhaps so. Perhaps that is what "reasonable" means. But it does not follow that there is a morally right balancing, in the sense in which there is a moral solution to the dilemma that occurs if a murder cannot be prevented without a lie. In that case, one commandment clearly overrides another. But overriding is not a relation that places all moral imperatives in a linear order.[9]

---

[8] *Dirty Hands*, Act VI, scene 2. In an interview about this play, Sartre said that its epigraph might very well have been the famous utterance of St. Just, "Nul gouverne innocemment." For a clever discussion of the entire concept from a political perspective, see Michael Walzer, "Political Action: The Problem of Dirty Hands," *Philosophy and Public Affairs*, II, no. 2 (1973), 160–80.

[9] Bas Van Frassen, "Values and the Heart's Command," *Journal of Philosophy*, LXX, no. 1 (1973), 11.

Van Frassen concludes that moral conflicts are possible and ultimate, that two sound and binding moral arguments may yield equally binding but quite incompatible conclusions, and that "the problem of possibly irresoluble moral conflicts reveals serious flaws in the philosophical and semantic foundations of 'orthodox' deontic logic." Deontic logic is too technical a subject to discuss here. But this formalistic translation of Sartre's dramatic intuition yields a serious argument against deriving an ethic, a system of coherent imperatives, from what is. For sound arguments with *factual* premises cannot yield true but incompatible conclusions. Should we get such conclusions, highflown talk about dialectical reasoning and linear discourse notwithstanding, one or another premise has to be false or ambiguous. Of course, the issue may be complicated when the premises are based not on the world *en-soi* but as it is for *us*. But then they are not simply factual, since moral considerations are inseparable from the structures of the world for us, and the derivations are not accordingly based on morally neutral grounds. Truths cannot conflict, but obligations can, and the inescapability of choice, to lapse again into Sartrian terminology, haunts the foundations of moral discourse.

# SARTRE'S LIFE:
# A BIOGRAPHICAL NOTE

"One can be productive without working all that hard," Sartre once modestly told an interviewer. "Three hours in the morning, three in the afternoon, that's my only rule." Six hours of literary labor every day, *même en voyage*, should entail that the biography of a man capable of such industry will be indiscernible from his bibliography. But though an unqualified intellectual, Sartre has been anything but a drudge, and his life appears to have been a vivid one, full of friendships and entanglements, loves and battles. And the volumes he is responsible for have not been confined to the sphere of literature: they have broken into life, reflecting and transforming the historical moments of their appearance to so great a degree as to be inseparable from history. The scholar intrepid enough to essay the definitive biography had better be prepared to write the history of France from World War II to the present. The bare *chronicle*, meanwhile, is roughly as follows.

## Sartre's Life: A Biographical Note | 164

Born in Paris in 1905 and left fatherless abruptly, Sartre was essentially raised by his maternal grandfather, Charles Schweitzer, a teacher of modern languages and particularly of German, in whose household he enjoyed, until her remarriage in 1916, an almost sibling relationship with his young widowed mother. It was a household in which intellectual and literary values were highly prized, and Sartre's infantine literary efforts were consequently reinforced by a doting approbation. He describes this atmosphere with a fond sardonic irony in *The Words*. Madame Sartre's second husband was actively loathed by her son, whose adolescent years were spiritually bitter, and the familial triangle seems strikingly to resemble the one between Baudelaire, his stepfather, and his mother, as described in Sartre's "psychoanalytical" study of that poet. In 1924 he entered the prestigious École Normale Supérieure, where he met Simone de Beauvoir in 1929. Their enduring liaison, a kind of reinvention of the marital relationship, is legendary. From 1931 to 1944 he taught philosophy at various *lycées*, first at Le Havre, which is identifiably the geopsychological model for Bouville in *Nausea*, and finally at the Lycée Condorcet in Paris, until his literary income enabled him to devote himself fully to writing.

Sartre's pedagogical career meanwhile was interrupted by the war. He was mobilized in 1939 and was taken prisoner (without having seen combat) in 1940. Characteristically, he wrote part of *The Age of Reason* and *Being and Nothingness* while a soldier, and while a prisoner of war wrote a Christmas play for his comrades, to whom he also taught Heidegger. (Wittgenstein, under similar circumstances of captivity, wrote the *Tractatus* a generation earlier.) In 1941, after his release, he formed with Maurice Merleau-Ponty an "intellectual resistance" group, and though clearly identified with the Resistance movement, he appears not to have engaged in any particularly dangerous actions. *Nausea* had been published in 1938, and *Being and Nothingness* appeared in 1943, *presque inaperçu*, according to Contat and Rybalka. *The Flies*, staged the same year, attracted rather more attention.

The year 1945 was a miraculous one: *No Exit* and the first two volumes of *Roads to Liberty* were published, as well as the first issue of his periodical *Les Temps Modernes*; Sartre gave his famous lecture *Existentialism is a Humanism*; he went twice to America, refused the Legion of Honor, lost his detested stepfather, and became world-famous. From 1946 until 1948, while giving innumerable conferences and lectures, Sartre wrote several plays, his study of Baudelaire, *What is Literature?*, the third volume of his novel, thus ending an extraordinary decade of productivity. *Saint Genet* appeared in 1961, *Critique de la raison dialectique: I* in 1959, and his massive soliloquy on Flaubert in 1970. Since 1948 Sartre has been tirelessly engaged in political and moral issues, a framer of petitions and manifestoes, unremittingly courageous and concerned. Increasingly disaffected with Soviet-style socialism and French communism, he has, after the *événements* of 1968 in Paris, been more and more identified with Maoist causes and publications. The definitive biography will be obliged to record his quarrels and affiliations with such major personages as Merleau-Ponty, Camus, Giacometti, and many others of only slightly lesser magnitude.

Sartre is short, square, tending toward corpulence, and wall-eyed. His striking ugliness notwithstanding, he is attractive to women and sexually successful. He eats and drinks copiously, though nothing raw, Simone de Beauvoir tells us with a kind of housewifely matter-offactness, and smokes incessantly. He feels at home, he confesses, only on the *cinquième étage* of a Parisian apartment house, and abhors the country. A witty, modest personality, Sartre is repelled by self-importance in others, and he is famous for his generosity. In his life as in his work, freedom is the dominating value. He never married, though he has an adopted daughter. "He has spent his adult life in a series of hotel rooms," Simone de Beauvoir said in an interview in 1946, "in which there is nothing of his own, not even a copy of his latest work, and which surprise visitors by their bareness." His disregard for material goods does not mean that he is ascetic, and his spontaneous independence does not make him a loner. He seems in the main to have been a happy person, and not to have felt guilty at being so.

# SHORT BIBLIOGRAPHY

I here list only works by Sartre in passable to good English translations, though not every such work. No published translation of the *Critique de la raison dialectique* yet exists, though substantial translated excerpts are in Cumming's anthology. Nor, to date, is there a translation of Sartre's massive study of Flaubert, *L'Idiot de la famille* (Paris: Gallimard: I and II, 1970; III, 1972). Readers equipped with French have available the exhaustive bibliography and chronology, through 1969, of Michel Contat and Michel Rybalka, *Les Ecrits de Sartre* (Paris: Gallimard, 1970). A splendid selection as well as a scintillating introduction to Sartre is by Robert Denoon Cumming, *The Philosophy of Jean-Paul Sartre* (New York: Random House, 1965); and a sensitive biography is by Philip Thody, *Sartre* (London: Studio Vista, 1971). A personal account of Sartre's life in the great period of his productivity is in Simone de Beauvoir's autobiographical volume *The Prime of Life*, trans. Peter Green (New York and Cleveland: World, 1962). I particularly recommend Germaine Brée's graciously written and singularly insightful portrait in her *Camus and Sartre: Crisis and Commitment* (New York: Delacorte, 1972).

## Short Bibliography | 168

PHILOSOPHICAL WRITINGS

*Being and Nothingness*, trans. Hazel Barnes. New York: Philosophical Library, 1956.
*The Emotions: Outline of a Theory*, trans. Bernard Frechtman. New York: Philosophical Library, 1948.
*Existentialism*, trans. Bernard Frechtman. New York: Philosophical Library, 1947.
*Imagination: A Psychological Critique*, trans. Forrest Williams. Ann Arbor: University of Michigan Press, 1962.
*Literary and Philosophical Essays*, trans. Annette Michelson. New York: Criterion Books, 1955.
*The Psychology of Imagination*, trans. Bernard Frechtman. New York: Philosophical Library, 1948.
*Search for a Method*, trans. Hazel Barnes. New York: Alfred A. Knopf, 1963.
*The Transcendence of the Ego*, trans. Forrest Williams and Robert Kirkpatrick. New York: Noonday Press, 1957.
*What is Literature?*, trans. Bernard Frechtman. New York: Harper & Row, 1965.


BIOGRAPHY AND AUTOBIOGRAPHY

*Baudelaire*, trans. Martin Turnell. New York: New Directions, 1950.
*Saint Genet, Actor and Martyr*, trans. Bernard Frechtman. New York: George Braziller, 1963.
*The Words*, trans. Bernard Frechtman. New York: George Braziller, 1964.


FICTION AND THEATER

*The Condemned of Altona*, trans. Sylvia and George Leeson. New York: Alfred A. Knopf, 1961.
*Dirty Hands*, in *Three Plays*, trans. Lionel Abel. New York: Alfred A. Knopf, 1949.
*Nausea*, trans. Lloyd Alexander. New York: New Directions, 1959.
*No Exit*, trans. Stuart Gilbert. New York: Alfred A. Knopf, 1946.
*Roads to Liberty*: I, *The Age of Reason*, and II, *The Re-*

*prieve*, trans. Eric Sutton. New York: Alfred A. Knopf, 1947; III, *Troubled Sleep*, trans. Gerard Hopkins. New York: Alfred A. Knopf, 1951.

*The Wall*, trans. Lloyd Alexander. New York: New Directions, 1948.

SOME WORKS IN ENGLISH OFFERING ALTERNATIVE VIEWS OF SARTRE

Grene, Marjorie. *Sartre*. New York: New Viewpoints, 1973.

Jameson, Frederic. *Sartre: The Origin of a Style*.

Murdoch, Iris. *Sartre: Romantic Rationalist*. New Haven: Yale University Press, 1953.

Olafson, Frederick A. *Principles and Persons*. Baltimore: Johns Hopkins University Press, 1967.

Warnock, Mary. *The Philosophy of Sartre*. London: Hutchinson, 1965.

———, ed. *Sartre: A Collection of Critical Essays*. New York: Anchor, 1971.

# INDEX

Absurdity 11, 12
Action, 96, 99–103, 137–38
Adventures, 2
Altruism, 105, 136
Anguish, 70–75; as antonym of seriousness, 76; and Bad Faith, 79ff; as "completely exceptional," 75–77; as consciousness of freedom, 73–75; and values, 153
Anselm of Canterbury, 10
Appearances, and reality, 46–47
Aristotle, 136
Aron, Raymond, 15, 16, 18
Art works, 28–31, 36
Authentic Existence, 27
Autodidact, 1

Austin, J. L., 32

Bad Faith, 22, 28, 74–81, 90, 123
Beauvoir, Simone de, 15, 16, 18, 21, 23, 147, 150, 163, 165
*Being and Nothingness*, 11, 26, 33, 37, 38, 47, 48, 51, 80–81, 82, 88, 109, 128, 132, 133, 134, 135, 147, 151, 156
*Being and Time*, 82–83
Bergson, Henri, 129
Berkeley, George, 16, 26, 41, 46, 47
*Bhagavad Gita*, 27, 104
Body, 98–103, 115, 118
Boredom, 63–64

Bourgeoisie, 22–23

Carroll, Lewis, 14
Camus, Albert, 130
Categorical Imperative, 131
Chestnut Tree, 4, 23
Choice, 145–46, 153
Consciousness, 16, 24–25, 34, 73–74, 96; as a form of deixis, 92–93; and its objects, 43, 58, 88; and nothingness, 68–69; of self and others, 115–118; and spontaneity, 66–68; structures of, Ch. II *passim*, 124–25. *See also* Pre-reflective consciousness
Conflict: as the essence of human relationships, 126, 131; between moral imperatives, 158–61
*Critique de la raison dialectique*, 3–4, 84, 106, 122, 132–36

*Dasein*, 89
Definition, importance of in philosophy, 40–41
Deixis, 92–93
Deontic logic, 161
Descartes, René, 45, 49, 98, 99, 101, 110, 112, 155
Description, 33–34
Determinism, 139
Destruction, 61–62
Diderot, Denis, 1

*Ding an sich*, 46, 86
*Dirty Hands*, 159–60
Distance, 92–93

Ego, 56–57
*Encyclopédie*, 1, 2
Engagement, Ch. III *passim*, esp. 88–89, 102; and literature, 31–32
*En soi*, 42, 51, 58, 59, 65, 69, 89
Essences: as contrasted with existence, 7–12, 25, 26; and freedom, 24
Existence, and consciousness, 55
Existence, Sartre's analysis of, 48–49, 59
"Existence precedes essence," 7, 25, 26
Existentialism, 25, 26; and humanism, 89; and marxism, 17–18, 86, 142
*Existentialism Is a Humanism*, 25, 164
Existential psychoanalysis, 16–17, 141, 142, 145
Explanation, 13–14
External World, problem of, 50

Facticity, 90–91
Faust, 27
$F(c) = c(F)$, 68–69, 73, 104
Flaubert, Gustave, 141–42
*Flies, The*, 37
Freewill controversy, 69–70

# Index

Freedom, 22, 24, 27, 36–37; and anguish, 73; as basic concept of Sartre's philosophy, 36–37; and determinism, 139–40; and facticity, 91–92; foundation of ours lies in others', 123–32, 140; and nothingness, 65–66; "paradox of," 139; and values, 147, 154–55
Futile Passion, 12, 95, 154
Freud, Sigmund, 142

Gambling, as an example of anguish, 72–73, 104
General Laws, Sartre's view of, 18–19, 20
Genet, Jean, 34
God, 10, 11, 90
Grace, 128–29
Groups, morphology of, 135–36; in-fusion, 135; serial, 135

Hare, R. H., 157
Hegel, Georg, 42, 46, 130
Heidegger, Martin, 12, 27, 61, 63–64, 74, 82, 83, 86, 89, 95, 134
"Hell is other people." 107–109, 120
Hintikka, Jaakko, 52
Human nature, 7, 25
Hume, David, 10, 11, 20, 56, 138, 143, 155
Husserl, Edmund, 15, 18, 56, 117

*Idiot de la famille, L'*, 17, 142
Imagination, 45–46
Intensionality, 43–45, 88, 110

Justification, of moral choices, 156–59

Kant, Immanuel, 9, 13, 39, 46, 48, 85, 86, 131, 152
Keats, John, 29
Kierkegaard, Sören, 75
Knowing that one knows, 51–52
Knowledge, of objects, 91–96

Lacks, 104, 105, 106, 138, 149, 154
Language, and reality, 1–2, 4–6, 14, 95–96
Locke, John, 49, 98
Looks, 121–22
Love, 126–28, 134

Malraux, André, 130
Marcel, Gabriel, 93, 100
Marxism, and Existentialism, 17–18, 86, 142
Merleau-Ponty, Maurice, 41, 85, 86, 97, 98, 99, 100, 101, 164
Metaethics, 148–51
Moral propositions, semantics of, 148–49
Morality, 136, 146, and Ch. V *passim*
*Morts sans sépulture*, 144
"My world," 118–21, 149

Nagel, Thomas, 105
Naming, 33
*Nausea*, Ch. I *passim*
Nausea, 4, 44, 48
Needs, 106
Negation, origin of, 61–62, 65–66
*Negatités*, 64, 149, 188
Negative facts, 60–61
Nietzsche, Friedrich, 21, 113, 116
Nihilation, 68–69
*No Exit*, 37, 51, 107–109, 125, 164
Noncognitivism, 149
Nothingness, 42, 57, 59, 62-63, 64, 65, 66, 68–69, 92–93, 149

Obscenity, 128–29
Ontological Argument, 10, 117
Ontology: and phenomenology, 38–41, 50; and values, 155–56
Original Choice, 137
Other Minds, Problem of, 112–16, 117, 118

"Paradox of freedom," 139–40
Performatives, 33
Phenomenology, 15–16, 38, 39, 41, 50, 86
"Pierre is not in the café," 62–64
Plato, 9, 29, 30, 40, 41, 46, 90

Poetry, 31–32
Positional consciousness, 54, 58
*Pour autrui*, 42, 55, 109–11
*Pour soi*, 41–42, 59, 69, 86, 87, 91, 103, 105, 115
Prereflective consciousness, 53–54, 55, 57, 58, 68–69, 70, 74, 75
Prereflective synthesis, 85–86
"presence," 93–95, 103-104
Prichard, H. A., 52
Prose, 32
Protagoras, 87
Pythagoras, 40

Qualities, 97, 143
Questioning, 60–61

Reading, 35–37
Real Definitions, 9, 13
Reality, Sartre's definition of, 16, 47–48, 120
Reasons, and causes, 137–138
Rimbaud, Arthur, 56
*Roads to Liberty*, 27, 37, 164
Russell, Bertrand, 40, 129
Ryle, Gilbert, 98

Sadism, 128–31
*Salauds*, 20
Sartre, Jean-Paul: his apoliticality before World War II, 23; his character, 164–65; his

liaison with Simone de Beauvoir, 127; his moral confidence, 153; his physical ugliness, 164; his productivity, xi, 162; systematic character of his philosophy, 24–25, 61
Scarcity, 132–34
Self-deception, 77–79
Self-reference, 114–15
Semantical Nihilism, 6
Seriousness, 21, 22, 76, 149, 156
Shame, 111–15, 122–24
Sidgwick, Henry, 105
Situations, 71, 86, 89, 123, 149
Socrates, 87
"Some of These Days," 28
Sorel, Georges, 136
Soul, 143
Speech, and action, 33
Spontaneity, 66–69, 71
Spinoza, 52, 126
Stopppard, Tom, 69
"Subjectivity is the starting point," 25, 26, 89
Superfluousness, 10–11, 12, 28
*Search for a Method*, 17

Temporality, 103–105
Third, the, 134

Torture, 129–30, 137, 144
Transcendence, 51
*Transcendence of the Ego*, 54, 56, 66, 70, 113

Ultimate Projects, 142–46
Unconscious, 52–53, 56, 57, 58, 141
Utilitiarianism, 159

Values, 147–56
Van Frassen, Bas, 160–61
Violence, 133
*Vorhanden*, 83, 84, 85, 86, 87, 101

Walzer, Michael, 160
"We," 134
"We are what we are not," 69
*What Is Literature?*, 31, 32–36
Will, 66–67
Wittgenstein, Ludwig, 5, 6, 90, 95, 150, 151
*Words, The*, 22, 163
Writing, 34–37

Yeats, W. B., 29
"You're free, choose!", 157–58

*Zeugganzes*, 84, 130
*Zuhanden*, 83, 84, 85, 86, 101